THE BLACK PROBLEM

Papers and Addresses on Various Native Problems

BY

D. D. T. JABAVU, B.A. (Lond.),

PROFESSOR OF BANTU LANGUAGES,
S.A. NATIVE COLLEGE, FORT HARE, ALICE, C.P.

NEGRO UNIVERSITIES PRESS
NEW YORK

Originally published in 1920
by The Book Department

Reprinted 1969 by
Negro Universities Press
A DIVISION OF GREENWOOD PUBLISHING CORP.
NEW YORK

SBN 8371-2030-6

TO MY WIFE
But for whose self-denial this volume would
not have been compiled.

" Ce n'est que le premier pas qui coûte."

PREFACE.

SO much has been said and written about the Native Problem of South Africa that any further intrusion into this vexed question seems to call for an explanation, if not, indeed, an apology. In offering this modest volume of speeches and addresses, the writer has been influenced by certain clearly defined motives.

In the first place, the times appeared to be ripe for the statement of a Native's opinions on Native matters. In connection with the progress through Parliament of that far-reaching measure the Native Affairs Act of 1920, much has been said in Parliament, on political platforms, at conferences and in the press on Native matters. While much enthusiasm, some meanness, and not a little race hatred have been shown, the prominent feature of these utterances has been the ignorance of Native opinion and Native ideals revealed by the speakers and writers. This has been largely inevitable since, through lack of opportunity, guidance and proper education, no Native has hitherto attempted a serious and comprehensive explication of the Native question. It is true that fragmentary statements have been made from time to time in the Native press and by certain organisations. We are still, however, unsupplied with an all-round practical exposition of the Native problem by a Native, an exposition that would constitute an adequate reference work, providing both negative and constructive criticism. This is part of the work essayed by the present volume.

In the second place it seemed necessary that the Native people themselves, should receive such friendly criticism and guidance as can be given to them by one of their own race. If it is true that it takes a Native to know a Native, the writer should be in an especially favourable position to advise his fellow countrymen, since it has been his task to study the languages of all the South African Native peoples, with their local, racial and social characteristics. He is conscious of their strength and weaknesses. And in several of the articles in the present volume he is addressing people whom he knows intimately, whose life is his life and whose problems are his problems.

The *post bellum* spirit is one of aggressive reconstruction. The world to-day in every sphere of activity, not excepting in churches and religion, wants practical men, preachers and prophets who, whilst seeing the faults in things and men as they are, stand by with remedies and solutions. It has no time for idle grumblers. The present booklet may not fully supply the contemplated need, but the author hopes it may indicate, for future Native African researchers, the way in which this may be done. One says designedly African researchers; for however sympathetic and good a European may be, he cannot undertake such a task with the minute knowledge and enthusiasm that can belong only to the Native African, who must himself be the victim of the untoward circumstances and difficulties under discussion.

In the third place, the black man is in danger of losing confidence in the possibility of good coming his way from the white man—indeed many think that he has already lost it irrevocably. The writer does not share this pessimism; but even if it were the case, it would still be possible, one would like to think, to restore this moribund confidence to life, provided that the black man can secure the right type of leader from his own race, to master his psychology and guide him aright in the difficult task of race-adjustment.

This work, being a compilation of papers and addresses made during the course of the last seven years, has a certain overlapping of topics due to the disconnection in the dates of the occasions that called forth the efforts. The repetition may, however, prove an advantage as it will serve to emphasise the more important points of the general Native question. Hence for those to whom the use of the first personal pronoun is a rock of offence, the writer should say in explanation that several of the addresses, far from being philosophic disquisitions, were simple talks to simple Native teachers, and frequently to unsophisticated rustics who appreciate the direct personal appeal better than impersonal abstractions.

References will be supplied, it is hoped, in the bibliography of a subsequent work, "The Bantu Tongues," for the purpose of those who would like to follow up some of the subjects to which brief allusion is here made.

Thanks are due to Rev. J. E. East of Middledrift, C.P., for to him and to a close association with him in social work among the rural people of our vicinity, I owe much of my information on agricultural matters and conditions. The formal addresses of the Native Farmers' Association included under the section on Agriculture are introduced here only because the writer was a collaborator in the framing thereof.

I am thankful to Rev. H. B. Coventry, B.D. (Lond.), of Lovedale, for his valuable assistance in the correction of many proofs and certain verbal suggestions, and to my College students for transcriptions and typing.

A word of gratitude is due also to Prof. Alexander Kerr, M.A., Principal of the S.A. Native College, for his generosity in granting me leave to attend meetings of farmers and teachers as well as religious conferences; for had it been withheld, as it could have been withheld *sine injuria*, this book would not have been possible.

To Dr. C. T. Loram, M.A., LL.B., Chief Inspector of Native Education, Natal, the author is deeply indebted for encouragement in the genesis of this venture. May it not be in vain.   D. D. T. J.

September, 1920.

CONTENTS.

Part 1.

NATIVE UNREST.

ITS CAUSE AND CURE.

(A paper read before the Natal Missionary Conference, Durban, July, 1920).

The Bantu people throughout the Union of South Africa are in a state of positive discontent. One need not be regarded as an alarmist for making such a statement. These people are, as it were, beginning to wake up out of their age-long slumber and to stretch themselves out and speak through their press and platform-demagogues in municipal areas like Johannesburg, Cape Town and Bloemfontein, their voice waxing louder and louder; while even in the rural districts of Natal, Pietersburg, the Transkeian reserves and among Free State squatters there is a growing feeling of distrust in the white man's lordship, loss of faith in his protestations of just intentions, and loss of confidence in the old-time kindly protection of the British Constitution. These feelings are largely not expressed, for the Native is not given to confiding the secrets of his inmost feelings to Europeans, as in many cases he dare not; but nevertheless the feelings are there, and are seething like molten volcanic lava in the breasts of these inarticulate people.

It is only the bolder spirits who have ventured to give the world this secret by means of their scathing criticism in their press (the *Abantu-Batho* of Johannesburg being the most outspoken organ), and through their deputations to Great Britain.

And unless something is done at once to mitigate the

1

causes of present dissatisfaction it will not be very long before the whole white community must deal with a situation overwhelmingly beyond their control.

1. The most immediate cause of unrest, although there are two or three more equally serious, and others less serious though individually and collectively serving to create an atmosphere of suspicion, the most immediate cause of unrest is the present economic pinch.

The Natives have been far harder hit by the prevailing high prices of the strictest necessities of life, than has been the white man. This needs no proving for the daily press reports unusual prosperity and extravagant spending of money by those who have made fortunes out of the high prices of merchandise. Government estimates display greatly increased salaries and wages; white employees and clerks everywhere are being paid in accordance with the times, either as a consequence of strikes, threatened strikes, or other persuasion. This is all due to the fact that the European, being well educated, knows how to speak out his sufferings, plead his case intelligently in the press, organise to the point of perfection, enlist public opinion in his cause, and finally force the hands of Government.

What about the black man? Behind him he has no European public opinion, the thing that counts in this country; for his power to influence it is negligible because three fourths of his fellowmen in the Union being without the franchise he has no political pull on Government. Hence he is expected to be satisfied with pre-war wages plus a rise of only five per cent. where the cost of living has advanced by from fifty up to a hundred per cent. The prices of rice and sugar are fixed; but maize, the staple food of millions of black people, is left to the mercy of speculators. A native labourer in East London recently asked in the "Dispatch" how he could be expected to be honest on a pound a week when

2

his food, rent and light alone cost him far more than that a week. The fact is that in most cases to-day the wages earned by a black man cannot buy his food and the barest needs of life. It should be remembered too that the labourers in the Rand and elsewhere are there to raise money not only for their personal needs but for the support of their people at home. Fireside discussions of these things are more rife than they have ever been before. The cure for this is the sympathetic revision of the scales of wages by employers everywhere, the alternative being that the blacks will be obliged to learn the methods of white trade-unionists and be gradually drawn into socialistic organisations to compel the employers to pay at their dictation, just as the American Negro has done who to-day receives 15s. a day for the same type of unskilled labour for which the Bantu get two shillings.

2. Successive droughts with failures of crops have rendered agriculture, on the lines of the ante-diluvian African cultivation, unprofitable, neglected and unpopular. Wonderful opportunities in this connection are being lost by the Union as a whole, for the Natives are capable of being made important factors in the development of production. On this point the Native Farmers' Association of Middledrift, C.P., last year prepared a memorandum for the Native Affairs Department where, however, it received no attention, a memorandum recommending the purchase of a farm by government in which Natives would be taught how to make a living out of an "isikonkwane" (six-acre plot), by means of a one-horse or one-ox American plough on the lines of Southern State negroes, to be taught by an American negro familiar with the system. Incidentally, dipping has produced much ill-feeling, for Natives do not understand its aim, and they ignorantly imagine it to be a white man's dodge to kill off their cattle, as witness the Mata-

3

tiele disturbances in 1914; and Natives value cattle above all their other worldly possessions. This is therefore a sore point with them. The cure here lies firstly in the educational training of headmen and chiefs who will encourage the pursuits of agriculture; secondly in the multiplication of native farm demonstrators on the American style to teach dry-farming methods; and thirdly in the establishment of agricultural schools for Natives; for it does not escape the knowledge of the more intelligent Native, that while government spends £100,000 yearly on agricultural schools for whites, plus overseas scholarships and experimental stations, it provides next to nothing for black people who pay the bulk of the taxes and stand in sorest need for this training.

3. In politics the black people are in the predicament of the American colonists of the eighteenth century who were taxed without representation. Whatever else has held good heretofore the time has gone past when the Bantu of this Union could be treated as children, however uneven be their development in the mass. They have vivid recollections of how their political rights were bargained away in the pacification of Vereeniging (1902). They reckon that the Union Act of 1910 unites only the white races and that as against the blacks; for the colour bar clause struck the death-knell of Native confidence in what used to be called British fair play. "That cow of Great Britain has now gone dry," they said, and they must look to themselves for salvation. All their deputations were referred back to the adjudication of the very government they appealed against and which had now by some dexterous manœuvre made itself its own final Court of Appeal! Then immediately after the achievement of Union the Dutch Reformed Church in her capacity as a Christian Church piloted through parliament in the teeth of glaring heterodoxy an act to

4

stamp herself indelibly as an anti-Native Church. Behold the contradiction in terms!

Out of this seed-bed of racial antipathy and out of a sense of self-preservation there sprang up several native and coloured political organisations, chief of which was the "South African Native National Congress," which to-day represents the strongest single volume of Native feeling in the Union, although its methods and spokesmen are open to criticism by certain sections of natives. The next thing which has probably done more than any other political event to rouse and antagonise Native feeling against whites is the passing of the 1913 Native Land Act. The irony of it is that the Act was engineered by a man long acknowledged as a great friend of natives, a friend who had to perform an odious task under the political whip hand of a refractory negrophobist section of the then government. Had Mr. Sauer lived to administer the Act he would in all probability have mitigated its hardships. As it was, he died immediately, and its rigour in the Orange Free State was and still is Procrustean, whatever may be said for it in other provinces; for in this province its effect was to dispossess and reduce the native to a veritable bondman. A lurid picture of its torments is to be found in "Native Life in South Africa," by S. Plaatje. Mr. Selby Msimang, the editor of a Bloemfontein Native paper, has collected a number of verifiable cases of its recent victims; while an eloquent sketch of the political position of Natives at that time may be seen in the "Dream of Alnaschar" speech by Dr. Abdurahman, a coloured political leader of Cape Town. Other political events that are factors in the present state of native unrest are (i) The 1914 Native deputation to the Imperial Parliament to appeal against the Lands Act. True, it returned fruitless, but its pertinacious labours have gone a long way in educating the British public on the political disabilities of the aborigines in this country. (ii) The 1918 Urban Areas Bill which sought to bestow unprecedented legislative powers upon town councils, including the power to create municipal beer canteens, the effect of which would have been to demoralise town natives. (iii) The Native Administration Bill of 1917 whose impracticability caused it to break in the hands of its own forgers. (iv) The 1918 Rand Strike of Native Sanitary labourers with the summary and notorious treatment they received at the hands of the local magistrate. This incident has served to unite Native miners because they have ever since been confirmed in the idea that Government favours white strikers but represses the black. As the late Mr. J. B. Moffat pointed out in his report this idea is a delusion so far as the law goes; nevertheless it remains in the Native mind and it is for the powers that be to eradicate it. (v) If ever one race in the world did ever seek the most signal way to repress and humiliate another, human invention could not have done it more effectually than the system of Pass Laws now obtaining in the Northern provinces. For decades, from the days of the Dutch Republics, has this system enslaved the Native, and the Union, instead of palliating its incidence, has not only continued it, accentuated it, but has actually threatened to make it universal or "uniform," to put it in the cunning language of the law-maker. This thing, as one man expressed it on the Reef, is simply perpetuated martial law in peace time.

The revulsion of Native feeling came to a head in a general Passive Resistance movement in Bloemfontein, Kroonstad, the Witwatersrand and elsewhere in 1918, when people mutually agreed to throw away these passes and undergo voluntary imprisonment. (vi) Particularly painful and distressing were these laws on women in the Free State and Natal.

Certain utterances by Europeans of eminence appearing from time to time in the press have further alienated many Native minds. Such are the words of the Johannesburg magistrate to the sanitary strikers. The famous Savoy speech by General Smuts in London in 1917 has remained an enigma to Natives of this land.

Remarks like those made by a Mr. Van Hees lately in parliament on justice being only for whites and not for blacks do a great deal of damage. Also, what does the expression "to make this a white man's country" mean? Whoever is responsible for coining it must have meant the repression and destruction of black races. (vii) The 1920 Native Affairs Bill is moving Natives who have studied it for two reasons: (a) No attempt has been made to consult them generally before it was framed or discussed in parliament, in view of the permanent character of the machinery it seeks to put up; (b) It has been feverishly rushed through parliament, just as was the Lands Act of 1913, which itself is now proclaimed as the first instalment of the Union Government policy. This feverish hurry has of itself engendered suspicion.

Its powers are so elastic that everything is going to depend upon the personnel of the commissioners; and it seems only fair that Natives should be consulted upon the choice of such plenipotentiaries. See also the "Grievances Memorial" pamphlet recently prepared by Messrs. Pelem and Soga, Queenstown, C.P.—perhaps the most comprehensive document, written by Natives of the Cape Province in exposition of the Native Question from the political point of view; the present writer did not see it until this paper had been completed.

4. In the Department of Justice the Native has gradually lost faith. i. In a country like South Africa, the jury system can never be a success inasmuch as it bolsters up the distortion of justice nurtured by racial hatred, and cloaks it over with an appearance of legal rectitude.

Even a tyro can tell that a black man in a country such as this can hardly expect fairplay from a white jury, when he is pitted against a white man. ii. The sentences of magistrates are a puzzle, and in their severity are distinctly anti-native. For the crime of failing to dip, a magistrate in Kafraria recently fined a Native £20, a fine indubitably disproportionate both to the offence, and the circumstances of the defendant, as compared with the same magistrate's fine against a European who had committed a similar offence. iii. Suspended sentences, as was remarked lately, in the House of Assembly by Mr. Langenhoven, seem to have been invented for the sole benefit of the European and to bear little or no reference to Natives. iv. Natives do not fail to notice that Europeans get off lightly and quietly in crimes against Natives, such as murder and rape, while Natives are unmistakably punished with the utmost rigour of the law amidst press trumpetings and fanfare. v. A high court Judge was not long ago reported in the "Daily Dispatch" as practising and upholding the differentiation of punishment as between whites and blacks for similar offences. Under these circumstances can one wonder that Natives should lose confidence in British Justice?

5. In social life the "School Native" cannot move anywhere without being made to know that his black skin is his life-long damnation. He is practically not recognised as a citizen entitled to a place under the sun, (particularly is this the case in Northern provinces). For instance in Pretoria I had three simple Post Office transactions to negotiate. I entered the main post office to buy stamps, for I saw several natives entering and being served. Peremptorily I was told in a discourteous and gruff manner, that Natives could not buy stamps there but had to go some two hundred yards round the

block of buildings to the next street, where after much search, I eventually discovered a back-kitchen sort of arrangement with Indian salesmen behind the counter, and got my stamps. To despatch my parcel to East London, I was told to go back to the General P.O. On getting there it was duly registered; and I desired to purchase a postal order, but was then told to travel back to the Native P.O. for that! My feelings are best left undescribed. Again when in Pretoria, I moved between friends at the East end of the town and others near the Indian bazaar, a distance of about two or three miles across town, covered directly by a 6d. tram ride. Being a black man I was not allowed to use the trams, and was compelled either to foot it daily all the way along the very tram route or pay half-a-crown each time for a private cab.

Socially speaking, the black man in all public places is either "jim-crowed" or altogether ostracized. In stores he has to wait until all whites are served; in public offices, he is bullied by officials; in markets his stock and produce are by tacit agreement earmarked for low prices; his sugar cane is not accepted at the Zululand mills; evening curfew bells restrict his freedom of movement among his friends and he is cut and snarled at throughout his life.

6. In railways he is at the very start of his journey buffeted by booking clerks; in the goods sheds he is unnecessarily anathematised in language that cannot bear repeating. His waiting rooms are made to accommodate the rawest blanketed heathen; and the more decent Native has either to use them and annex vermin or to do without shelter in biting wintry weather. His accommodation in trains is frequently not equal to the money he pays in fares.

To travel 3rd class is often a test of physical endurance

9

specially on some lines where there are more people than the half coach or single coach can contain. Travelling first class from Alice to Durban recently my first class compartment was in many cases only an old second redubbed "First" and, as it was, I was recklessly dumped with second class passengers—the very privacy for which I had paid being denied. Reserved bookings by Natives are frequently ignored. Several times have I had to claim refunds from railway divisional superintendents when after fulfilling all legal requirements for reserving a seat, I had to go third or not go at all. A number of Native teachers last winter wrote to Umtata a fortnight ahead of time to have second class seats reserved for them. When they came to join the train not only was there no accommodation made for them but no second class tickets would be issued to them and they had either to abandon travelling or go third class. When I joined the same train at Butterworth I was offered pretty much the same treatment, but I stood my ground, threatening to take legal proceedings against the delinquents when after half an hour's palaver an extra coach was attached, to the relief and joy of many black passengers who included a native doctor qualified in Edinburgh University. Such incidents often render railway travelling a perfect misery, as the decent Native has constantly to engage in ugly altercations with supercilious officials in claiming his privileges. Much heartburning has come from the system of replacing blacks by poor whites in railway sheds and workshops. Refreshment stalls like those at Amabele, Komgha and Sihota are doing incalculable harm, converting otherwise peaceful natives into bitter malcontents by their disgusting contempt for native passengers in peculiarly native districts. In fact Transkeian Europeans by their policy of pin-pricks against natives are gradually accentuating racialism. For example rank prejudice is shown in the

10

very Council Hall at Umtata where Natives may use only a certain door to enter or leave the hall in the Bunga sessions, this piece of snobbery even necessitating crossing the hall in front of the magisterial benches—all this in a Native reserve.

The cure here lies in the appointment of officials with tested sympathy towards Natives, in all departments of Government.

The above six points constitute, in my view, the most important factors in the general ferment of unrest, which need urgent solution. Now I wish to take eight other points which contribute not a little to the charged atmosphere that has been electrified by racial distrust.

7. Native Housing: This question deserves the attention of all interested in the welfare of Natives. In most municipalities these people live in squalid surroundings, shockingly overcrowded, these quarters being favourable breeding beds for disease and epidemics. From their nature they are cesspools of drunkenness and demoralisation. Conveniences are distant, sometimes non-existent; water is hard to get; light is little; sanitation bad; while there are no common laundry buildings, no gardens, no amusement halls or clubs. Some are located near sanitary dumps, e.g. Klipspruit and Springs in the Rand. The favourite solution of the problem is to threaten to remove them further away from the towns without promising improvement of conditions.

The cure for this is to be found in the suggestions made in the newly-published Government Commission Report on Housing. Many constructive proposals may be gained also from the speech of Mr. P. D. Cluver, Mayor of Stellenbosch, given at Grahamstown in the 1920 Municipal Congress and from the "Municipal Control of Locations," a paper by Dr. F. A. Saunders, F.R.C.S., of Grahamstown (now published in pamphlet form) delivered before the same Congress.

11

8. Insecurity of land tenure: Like the owning of cattle the possession of land, to Natives, is a natural ambition. But the possibility to buy land or hire it has been seriously circumscribed everywhere by the Lands Act of 1913. The worst case is that of the Orange Free State which has rendered confusion for the black man worse confounded. Before 1913 the Native could hire land or plough on the half-share system for a white master and could not purchase land under any conditions. Today he is not allowed under this law to hire land or to contract to plough on half-shares. He is a literal serf, landless, unable to hire land, and must only be a paid servant of the Dutchman.

Also in many urban locations there are no facilities for Natives to buy property, hence there is no inducement for them to beautify, and improve with gardens, even if they did feel so inclined, the property that is rented from a town council and liable at any time to be moved away by a resolution of the town council.

9. Missions. Missionaries will for ever be remembered with gratitude by Natives as the people who befriended them in times of trouble and danger at the risk of their own lives. They faced opprobrium for the sake of black people, founded countless mission stations and bequeathed unto them the present foundations of their entire educational structure that is to-day theirs. Today however there is a danger· that the type of earnest missionaries associated with the founders of prominent mission stations and Native Training Institutions is being steadily replaced by ministers and other staff members of a more and more secular spirit, who not only fail to understand the Native, much less to love him, but adopt a socially distant attitude of master to servant. Success in Christian work without Christian love is an impossibility. Now many a missionary of to-day has no

12

hand-shake for a black brother and he feels distinctly embarassed when he is among other whites and meets him in town.

His position is lordly, his discipline military. These doubtless form a small fraction of the whole but as in all things in the world, the many are apt to be judged by the few erratic cases. On one occasion I was invited by a Principal of a Native Training Institution to lecture to his students. He, as my host, took no steps to let me even see the inside of his house—perhaps with all my ten years of English University life I was not good enough for him—but boarded me among the boys in their dining hall where he only came to say prayers and to depart. There was high feeling among the boys and Native Teachers over this treatment of me but I asked them earnestly to say nothing about it for the day of Nemesis was bound to come since this attitude was characteristic of certain missionaries. Without delay Nemesis came within a few months afterwards.

One mentions this incident as a warning to a Conference of this kind for this is where racial sectarianism takes its source, for even in synods, presbyteries and conferences the spirit of racial discrimination is so powerful that the black delegates have again and again to be sorted out from the rest like goats from the sheep. Therefore do not rest on your laurels for Natives are watching you at every step. Their docility does not spell stupidity.

10. Education. The present condition of Native education in the Union is one of chaos, for while at the Cape and Natal there are signs of organisation to improve things, there is nothing of the sort being done in Transvaal and the Free State. Natives here have a just grievance. They see Government spending lavishly in putting up majestic educational edifices for European

primary, secondary and University education staffed by highly paid teachers, while they have to be satisfied with having their children taught in mission rooms with walls dilapidated and furniture rough and scanty, teachers receiving miserable pittances, so miserable that a raw and illiterate Zulu policeman in Durban today gets better pay than the best paid Zulu school teacher. Provincial grants to Native education are very tiny by comparison with those for white schools and infinitesimal as compared with the enormous revenue derived from Native taxation. There is no pension for a Native teacher in Natal.

The inspectoral system there however is a model one and a contrast to that of the Cape, where its terrorism over teacher and pupil is such that at a certain school near King William's Town the inspector not long ago actually failed an entire school of seventy, passing only four. Such a system needs overhauling. Cape Native teachers would be considerably benefitted in their work by an instructive and sympathetic, even humorous paper like the Natal Native Teachers' Journal published by the Education Department instead of the lifeless dry-bones of the Cape "Education Gazette."

The report of the Native Education Commission 1919 is a capital document worth studying as it contains valuable proposals, which would change a great deal of what is antiquated, if acted upon.

Useful for Cape Teachers would be Winter School courses such as those yearly organised in Natal by Dr. C. T. Loran, M.A., author of " The Education of the South African Native."

11. The Civil Service is greatly injuring Native sentiment with its policy of weeding out competent Natives where they can serve their people better than can other people. Even in a Native reserve like the

Transkei Terrirories, Native youths with good qualifications are put on a special Native scale of salaries lower than that of whites with inferior credentials. Why not give the Native a fair chance in his own reserve? Why must he after due training have to work under an inferior "black scale" of remuneration in a Native district? Why not give us a chance to rise according to our ability and professional qualifications? Such questions are being asked by people who wield no small influence among the less enlightened.

12. Bolshevism and its nihilistic doctrines are enlisting many Natives up-countries. Socialism of the worst calibre is claiming our people. The main alarming features are (a) That Christianity must be opposed and rooted out, for it is a white man's religion which the white man himself does not act upon. "Let us fabricate a religion of our own, an original, independent African religion suited to our needs, such as for instance, Mohamedanism, the great African faith," say they. (b) "Let us unite to compass our freedom, opposing the white man tooth and nail as he has taken our country and made us economic slaves." The cure here is that we should have in this country counteracting forces. There should be more social workers such as Dr. D. Bridgman and Rev. Ray Phillips in Johannesburg who are organising for Natives a sort of Y.M.C.A. scheme to provide recreation, a large club with reading, writing and restaurant rooms plus playing fields, debating and musical societies. This is needed in every location, rural and urban, to heighten the tone of Native life.

13. Agitators. There has sprung into life a large number of Natives from the better educated class who have seized the opportunity of the general state of dissatisfaction to stir up the populace to desperate acts. A sensational report of something of this kind

15

appeared in the vernacular in a recent issue of "Imvo" by a Rand correspondent. Personally I do not blame these men for the conditions that have called them into being are positively heartrending and exasperating in all conscience. They poignantly feel the sting of the everlasting stigma of having to carry passes in time of peace in the land of their birth. They are landless, voteless, helots; pariahs, social outcasts in their fatherland with no future in any path of life. Of all the blessings of this world they see that the white man has everything, they nothing.

Like Catiline and his conspirators of Roman history, they believe that any general commotion, subversion of government and revolution are likely, out of the consequent ruins and ashes, to produce personal gain and general benefit to Natives and sure release out of the present state of bondage. They harp upon the cryptic and dangerous phrase " to make this a white man's country," which as we all know has become Parliamentary platitude. Armed with rallying catch phrases and a copious Socialistic vocabulary they play as easily as on a piano upon the hearts of the illiterate minelabourers. It must be remembered too that the Socialism they acquire is not the harmless commonsense system advocated by Phillip Snowden and Ramsay Macdonald in their books; but the atheistic and revolutionist doctrines of Count Henri Saint Simon of the early 19th century introduced into England by Robert Blatchford, Charles Bradlaugh and J. M. Robertson in latter days, and now somehow imported into South Africa.

The cure here lies in our being able to produce well educated Native leaders trained in a favourable atmosphere, who will be endowed with commonsense, cool heads, with a sense of responsibility, endurance and correct perspective in all things. The Native

16

College at Fort Hare has this as one of its aims and if sufficiently supported it ought to be a real help to the country and the government.

14. Finally the Native Labour Contingent that did work in France during the Great War has imported into this country a new sense of racial unity and amity quite unknown heretofore among our Bantu races. Common hardships in a common camp have brought them into close relation. They had a glimpse at Europe and even from the closed compounds they got to discover that the white man overseas still loves the black man as his own child, while on the contrary some of their white officers, including two chaplains forsooth, made themselves notorious by their harsh treatment and slanderous repression of them when French people befriended them. All this was carefully noted and published in this country when they returned. The result is that there is among the diversified Bantu tribes of this land a tendency towards complete mutual respect and love founded upon the unhealthy basis of an anti-white sentiment. They thus provide plastic material for all sorts of leaders and agitators who may use it for good or ill.

It is the duty then of every loyal citizen of the Union to be familiar with these causes of unrest and discontent, with a view to each one taking his share in providing a solution that will save the country from what will, if not arrested in time, surely come up sooner or later as an anarchist disruption of this land.

PASS LAWS.

[Evidence of the Native Farmers' Association of the Eastern Province, before the Union Government Pass Laws Commission sitting in King Williams' Town, February, 1920.]

I. *Introductory.* In view of the liberty enjoyed by Cape Natives for the past century, and of the great progress they have made in civilisation, and of the fact that they have never abused the privileges bestowed upon them through this liberty, our feeling, as a Native Farmers' Association, is that it would be a retrograde step at this period of time to introduce and impose upon them the notorious up-country Pass system in however mild or modified a form. The system is both uncalled for and unnecessary, for crime has not only been not excessive in the most populous Native districts but has positively been below normal, as is year by year unsolicitously observed in the judicial circuit assizes by High Court judges. This province being admittedly and justifiably the most generous in its treatment of the aborigines should rather lead the Union—in fact this was the expectation at the foundation of Union,—in questions of Native policy than be led by, and follow in, the wake of the ill-reputed Transvaal regime.

II. *Objections.* In our opinion the Transvaal system of Pass Laws will be seriously objectionable for the following reasons:—

(a) The humiliation and personal inconvenience entailed by being liable by day and by night, abroad and indoors, to be harassed, examined and called upon by officials, in many cases ungentle officials, to produce passes.

(b) However reasonable and innocent the system may be made to appear, its administration by sub-officials has invariably produced, and certainly will continue to produce, an acerbity that rankles in the hearts of Natives.

18

(c) The additional taxation that the system must necessitate will greatly increase the already excessive burden of taxation under which the Native is groaning; for in many cases it actually reaches £4 per head, including school dues, with many Natives in the Cis-Kei.

(d) We Natives feel strongly that we are being unduly stigmatised for being black people, as these laws apply only to us and not to Europeans, Coloureds and Asiatics.

(e) We object to any levelling up or uniformity of a Pass system of the Union that would lower, as this will certainly lower, the status of the Native in the Cape Province. For the Pass system is inherently a relic of barbarism, a sort of martial law indubitably not necessary for the peaceful and law-abiding Native inhabitants of the Cape.

III. *Constructive Suggestions.* (a) The system in vogue in the Cape whereby the better class Natives travel freely, unmolested and without passes, while the lower class are required to carry a pass when moving in places where they are unknown, seems to be the most civil and appropriate for all concerned.

(b) Failing this we would suggest that tax-receipts constitute a sufficient form of identification and adequate substitute for passes.

(c) Or some sort of universal manhood registration for all males, European and non-European, such as obtains in conscription countries in Europe.

(d) No charges under any circumstances should be made for passes, as this will surely lead Natives to believe that the system is introduced to exact revenue from the blacks.

A LOCATION SELF-TAXATION SCHEME.

Suggested to the Government by the Native Farmers'
Association, 3rd December, 1919.

To the Secretary,
> Department of Native Affairs,
> > Union Buildings, Pretoria.

Sir,

The Native Farmers' Association convey to you and
your department its deepest thanks for your communica-
tion of the 9th October last in which you gave
a reply to our enquiries about the working of the
Transvaal Tribal Trust Funds system of self-taxa-
tion and in which you concluded with the benevolent
and encouraging remark that your department "Is not
tied to any particular scheme; but any proposals bodies
of natives may put forward for co-operation amongst
themselves for their mutual assistance and progress will
be sympathetically entertained by this department, and
if found practicable the department will render every
assistance in its power."

In pursuance of this generous invitation and in view
of the fact that large numbers of native people live in
community groups and are congregated in some common place similar to municipalities, and have common
needs in the way of, for instance, water, wood, lighting,
education, dipping tanks, commonage-fencing, just as do
municipal corporations, the lack of which seriously im-
pedes their progress towards civilisation and at the same
time endangers their health, and in view of the fact that
finance is needed to meet the above requirements, we,
as an association, humbly beg to submit the following
scheme as one that might be found workable for natives
in our districts :—

That legislation be enacted or a proclamation be made
whereby :   (1) Natives living in a location be empowered

20

by a majority-vote of their own taxpayers to tax themselves with the object of securing any one or more of the following advantages: water-furrows, dams, lighting, education, dipping tanks, commonage-fencing, machinery benefit, the option to accept or reject the scheme to rest with each individual location or village.

(2) If a two-thirds majority-vote of taxpayers accept the scheme, then the law to enforce it upon all.

(3) The rate of tax to be imposed must be fixed by a majority-vote in the location concerned, after which it will be legally compulsory.

(4) The tax to be paid in to the existing Government offices along with the usual hut tax.

(5) A committee appointed by ratepayers of the location that accepts the scheme will administer the funds subject to the approval of the Native Affairs Department.

(6) Government to keep a set of books that shall show a separate account of revenue and expenditure of this special tax for each location.

(7) Each location to administer its funds independently and separately, that is, without reference to any other location, money raised under this scheme being expended only on that location's requirements and not any other.

(8) Money raised in this way cannot be borrowed, nor can it be used for any other object except that specified in the proclamation.

(9) It shall be the option of each location to increase or diminish the rate of its special tax, according to the specific needs of the same location.

(10) But if any money be raised by loan for the use of on any location to carry out any special purpose then there shall be no reduction in the rate of special tax until such loan be satisfied.

(11) The accounts and books of money raised in any location will be open to inspection by the ratepayers of that location.

(12) A managing board of five men, including the headman, shall be elected by the ratepayers of any location accepting the scheme and its duty shall be to administer the funds.

NATIVE AFFAIRS BILL.

VIEWS OF NATIVES.

A call meeting of the Native Farmers' Association was convened on the 12th June to consider and express opinions on the Native Affairs Bill. The great and statesmanlike speech of General Smuts wherewith he introduced the second reading of the Bill in Parliament was perused and translated. The Bill itself and also the Premier's speech that closed the debate were read and interpreted. Then an interval was given for the members to consider same and to draw up questions or comments in writing relative thereto.

We hereunder give some of the questions asked which the Hon. Secretary (D. D. T. Jabavu) attempted to answer :—

Question 1.—In view of the Premier's opinion on the 1913 Lands Act that it was too much hay on their forks and that the people of South Africa were not ready for it, does he then favour the repeal of the Act ?

Answer : I do not think so, for he seemed to justify it in his closing speech.

Q. 2.—What success is this that is claimed for the Glen Grey Act ?

A. : The Premier said it gave every satisfaction, and that the whole white community of this country held the Bhunga to be the panacea for all Native ills.

Q. 3.—From what you have gathered in travelling among Natives, do the Natives in Transkei say that the Bhunga is a success?

A.: No. I have here with me documentary evidence showing that the Natives there are greatly dissatisfied with it for the following reasons :—

(a) That the Natives have not the privilege of selecting Native men of their own choice specially in the unsurveyed districts; (b) that the magistrates unduly revise the decisions and recommendations of the Bhunga, this being regarded as the greatest weakness of their Council system; (c) there is a tacit, if not statutory, colour-bar to the advance of Natives to the higher positions of clerkship, etc., the remunerative positions being reserved for whites only ; this creates a bad impression on Native taxpayers ; (d) the Natives have no control over the expenditure of their revenue, for after the estimates are passed the magistrates in a special conclave of their own change and subtract anything they like ; (e) proclamations are issued *ad infinitum*.

Q. 4.—In his speech the Premier says the Councils will be applied optionally. Why does he not say that in the Bill?

A.: I do not know; the Bill does not say it will be forced on anybody, but the Government seems to reserve the power to proclaim it.

Q. 5.—Where in this Bill does the Premier seek to remove the stigma that the Natives have no political outlet, since the Commissioners and Councillors are to be appointed by the Governor-General.

A.: I do not know.

Q. 6.—Who will advise the Governor-General on the selection of these Commissioners?

A.: I think the Government, *i.e.*, the Minister for Native Affairs.

23

Q. 7.—Then the personnel of the Commission will depend upon the kind of men suggested by Government? A.: I think so.

Q. 8.—Is there any likelihood then of the present Government being changed?

A: Yes, quite. In fact Government was recently almost defeated and changed, the Nationalists being the rival party.

Q. 9.—What kind of a Commission would be recommended to the Governor General if General Hertzog's party got hold of the reins of Government?

A.: I fear the consequences.

Q. 10.—Cannot the Bill be so framed as to safeguard Native rights against anti-Native political parties?

A.: I think so; but what would you suggest? Here a suggestion was made that the Native people themselves should elect these Commissioners.

Q. 11.—Will any of the Commissioners be Natives?

A.: The Bill is silent on this point.

Q. 12.—Are we right in taking it that the successful operation of this Act will ultimately depend upon the acceptance of the recommendations from the Commission by the Minister, the Governor General and Parliament in return? A.: Yes.

Q. 13.—And in Parliament the Natives have no voice?

A.: No. There is the colour bar in the Constitution.

Q. 14.—Then the Bill does not go far towards removing the vital cause of Native unrest? A.: I cannot say.

Q. 15.—Could not fencing, afforestation and stud-stock be included under Section 6?

A: Yes, we may include those in our recommendations, to be numbered i, j, k.

Q. 16.—How large are the areas of the proposed Councils? A.: The Bill does not say.

Q. 17.—What is the standard qualification for those elected as members of the Council?

A.: The Government will fix that.

At this juncture the meeting again adjourned to enable a Committee to formulate recommendations and comments based upon the questions and discussion. The following suggestions were adopted :—

(1) Knowing as we do the great degree of distrust and unrest prevalent in the minds of the Natives, we fear that greater misunderstanding will be created if the Act is forced upon them; while on the contrary they will not accept it voluntarily, as in their present state of mind they deeply suspect anything, good or bad, that the white man offers them. While we very much regret this condition of mind among Natives, we feel that to conceal it would be calamitous. It is our opinion that the optional acceptance would have met with greater success had the Government accepted a number of Natives who command the confidence of the Bantu people to act with them in the framing of the Bill.

(2) We feel that in the electing of the Commissioners and Councillors the Government would have a splendid opportunity of giving the Native people the first step in the use of the franchise. At the same time this would safeguard the Native people from the recommendations of some future Government that may prove unsympathetic.

(3) It is our opinion that the smaller the areas of these Councils the greater will be their success, because people of different locations vary so much in their intelligence, aspirations and industriousness. When backward locations are combined with progressive locations, the result is bound to be detrimental to the latter, while if the progressive location had its own Council it could go forward as rapidly as it wishes, thus being an example stimulating lethargic locations. Again the natural resources and advantages of locations differ, and therefore require different rates of taxation, e.g.

25

some need afforestation whereas others are contiguous to natural forests. Some can irrigate their lands by gravitation, where others would invest in a windmill or machine pump.

One location that cannot utilise the gravitation scheme would not tax themselves to benefit another that could.

(4) Under section 6, following clause (h) we would recommend the addition of ; (i) fencing ; (j) afforestation ; (k) stud-stock.

(5) The inclusion, we think, of at least one Native among the Commissioners would go a long way to secure the confidence of the Natives.

(6) In view of the harsh administration of some unsympathetic resident magistrates in preponderantly Native districts, we would strongly recommend that the power to appoint magistrates be transferred to the Native Affairs Department, who will act on the advice of the Native Commission. Accession to this request would remove the radical cause of grave unrest among Natives. Also, Natives should have complete control over the expenditure of revenue in their Councils.

(7) Generally speaking we feel very grateful to the Prime Minister for the honest endeavour manifested in the conception of this measure and his noble and statesmanlike address in introducing it. Further we feel that if the spirit evinced in his speech be carried into practical effect, this will constitute a new and acceptable departure in Native administration. Our feeling is that the Bill, if suitably amended in its committee stage to meet Native aspirations, and if properly administered, will by far eclipse the present General Council system in the Transkeian Territories.

Part 2.

BOOKER T. WASHINGTON.

What he would do if he were in South Africa.

When the present writer in June, 1913, undertook a
a visit to the Tuskegee Normal and Industrial Institute,
Alabama, U.S.A., at the advice and with the help of
several good friends in England, for the purpose of
studying the methods and organisation of that famous
school, with special reference as to their applicability to
the peculiar circumstances of Natives in South Africa,
he received during September, 1913, a cablegram from
the Minister for Native Affairs, Union Government of
South Africa, requiring him to "furnish a full report on
the Tuskegee curricular and educational methods, including the elementary, practical and agricultural, with
views on their suitability and adaptability to the conditions of the Natives under the Union."

This report was duly submitted by October, and the
then Secretary of Native Affairs, the late Mr. Edward
Dower, intimated to me that Government intended to put
it into Blue Book form. Unfortunately the sky of European
politics darkened, and with the outbreak of the world
war the report was shelved for so long that when I made
inquiries this year I was informed that the Department
had no intention to publish it and that I was free to
utilise it in any way I chose.

Now, in view of the many changes that are taking
place in connection with Native Education in the Cape

Province, where an epoch-making commission was appointed in June, 1919, by the Administrator, Sir Frederic de Waal, presided over by Dr. W. J. Viljoen, whose wonderful report thereof has recently been published, and in Natal, where the Department of Native Education, under the guidance of Dr. C. T. Loram, is also introducing many welcome schemes, it seemed to me that the time had surely come that this report, whatever it may be worth, should see the light of day. Especially so because in both of the provinces above mentioned the the ideas and methods of Booker Washington seem to be known in a vague and general way from his book "Up from Slavery," and perhaps one or two others of his twelve volumes reviewed at the end of this section. Nobody, however, so far as one can make out, seems to be in possession of intimate and detailed knowledge of the inside working of that remarkable school of Tuskegee. And the report, if published in full, would really need to constitute a volume of itself. Hence for the present purpose, whilst awaiting the proper opportunity to publish it in full, I propose to incorporate here only its essential features, which should be a sufficient guidance for any school organiser desiring to put Washington's system into practical application.

At the outset it should be remarked that it is far harder to guess what Booker Washington would have done had he been in South Africa than to detail what he has actually accomplished in America. Here are many factors, knowable and unknowable, that make it well-nigh impossible to answer the question that heads this section. Nevertheless we have felt that an accurate description of what Washington has done in Tuskegee, together with tentative suggestions as to what can be done here, must be the best approximation of a satisfactory answer.

My stay at Tuskegee gave me the advantages of seeing the school in all its most important activities: the normal work of all the students; the Summer School arrangements which attracted over 400 teachers from various States, some extension work in the neighbouring rural districts, as well as the Negro organizations which utilise the Institute establishment for their conferences, as also the industrial and agricultural occupations of the students during vacation.

The scheme here adopted falls into the following sections: A.—A digest and analysis of the Tuskegee syllabus as from the "Annual Catalogue," or calendar, as we would term it, with comments and suggestions made step by step as to the possibility of the adaptation of such methods in South Africa; and General Remarks on the Syllabus.

B.—An index to the above suggestions and recommendations.

C.—General Impressions of Tuskegee.

D.—Booker T. Washington—a brief character sketch, with short reviews of all his books. Sections C. and D. formed the appendix in the original.

In my task I was incalculably indebted to the advice of many members of the Tuskegee Staff, who at all times gave me cheering and cheerful assistance, displaying all along the line the famous "Tuskegee spirit."

PRELIMINARY.

In comparing British educational systems with the American there is an initial difficulty, for the Britisher, of finding out the approximate value of the American School grades.

29

British schools have Standard IV (or Grade IV or Form IV), a definite unit the meaning of which is fairly well understood. This uniformity is convenient and valuable to one who has in mind the mystifying grades in American institutions, where to "matriculate" may mean much or little according to the particular school, college, or university. On this point, the following remarks, taken, "passim," from the "Report of the Commissioner of Education" for the United States Bureau of Education 1913, are pregnant :—

"Not all institutions calling themselves colleges or universities are listed as such in this report. Many of them do little or no work above the high-school grade ; some do little above the grade of the elementary school.

Again, in discussing teachers, the limited supply of them, their inefficiency as individuals and the inadequacy of teacher training in the United States, "It must be borne in mind that for various historical reasons the sense of public responsibility in the matter of education has developed unequally in different sections of the country. Standards of the teaching profession are much higher in some States than in others, and in most States the cities are far ahead of the country districts in adequate salaries and other conditions requisite for an efficient teaching force. It is simply that the State, in its eagerness to allow the maximum of local self-government has been reluctant to insist upon education as a State function. The first step in educational progress is recognition by the State of its direct school obligations ; once these are recognized in the form of ample financial support where such has hitherto been withheld, the public-school system of a particular section will improve sufficiently to make the national showing for education more nearly what it should be."

"A further complication is introduced by the extraordinary number of collegiate and university institutions which have the power to grant degrees, and do this on standards and courses so various as almost to defy reliable comparison between the scholars they turn out." [Prof. Parkin, administrator of the Rhodes Trust, London, speaking on the uncertain status of United States schools.]

It may be taken for granted that this elusive character of classification holds equally good with Negro educational organizations which are even more handicapped in the matter of well-equipped teachers. The history of the last ten years or more shows, however, that the standard of education everywhere in the States is advancing gradually and consistently.

In a Normal and Industrial institute like Tuskegee, where students spend three days of the week in the classroom and the three, alternately, at their trade, it is awkward, if not impossible, to get at the precise value of the academic standard and to express same in the terminology of British schools. It stands to reason that a Tuskegee student who spends one of his two school days in brickmasonry cannot be academically consider-ed alongside the Healdtown boy who remains in the classroom for both days. On the other hand the Tuskegee graduate and fully-fledged harnessmaker not only can earn more, in the struggle for life, than the Blythswood third year pupil teacher who knows more history and poetry, but is a more independent man on account of the independent character of his trade, which, in turn, brings him into vital touch with both the cultured and backward classes of his community.

Therefore in translating the Tuskegee Grades into English Forms I have endeavoured to keep in mind and counterbalance the academic differences in favour of the latter by the gain in industrial training.

31

THE SYLLABUS. I.

AIM AND METHOD.

The object of the Tuskegeee Institute is to provide young coloured men and women an opportunity to learn a vocation, and to gain a sound, moral, literary and industrial training, so that when they leave the school they may, by example and leadership, help to change and improve the moral and industrial condition of the ccmmunities in which they live.

The methods of instruction employed aim to correlate and combine the academic studies and industrial training in such a way as to emphasize the social and moral significance of skilled labour and at the same time illustrate, in the shop and in the field, the practical meaning of the more abstract teaching of the class room. And there are at least ten sets of literary, debating or temperance societies of one kind or other, all remarkably well utilized by the scholars. Equally patronised are the five voluntary religious organizations maintained by the students : Young Men's Christian Association, Young People's Society of Christian Endeavor, The Young Women's Christian Temperance Union, The Young Women's Christian Association, and the Edna D. Cheney Missionary Society.

The combination of these with the Chapel and other devotional exercises constitutes a religious system unsurpassed, for versatility, even by some avowedly missionary institutions.

SCHOOL PUBLICATIONS.

The "Tuskegee Student" is a bi-monthlv newspaper devoted to the interest of students, teachers and graduates.

The "Southern Letter," a monthly publication, is a record of the work of the graduates and former students and goes to persons outside the school who are interested in its work.

The "Messenger" is a county newspaper for the encouragement of the work in the public schools of the county and for instruction of the farming community in agriculture, and is published under the direction of the Extension Department.

MILITARY TRAINING.

Here follows the subject of Military training, which we do not propose to explain as under the South African Union Defence Laws, it is not likely to be countenanced. As a substitute for it however one would recommend the system advocated by Mr. W. C. Atkins, M.Sc., of Adams M.S., Amanzimtoti, N., and Rev. Ray Phillps, B.A., B.D., of American Zulu Mission, Johannesburg, on the "Laws of the Pathfinders" and "Scouting for Boys."

ADMISSION OF STUDENTS.

The standard of admission is, in our own grading, about the third or the fourth or between those two,

EXPENSES.

The necessary expenses of a student at Tuskegee are small. It is intended, so far as possible, that no diligent, worthy student shall leave the Institution because of a lack of means.

Tuition is free to all students. Charges for board. etc., are :

Entrance fee	...	...	...	£2
Board per month	...	...	...	£2

Day School students are given an opportunity to work out from 6s. to 12s. per month on their board, thus leaving from 24s. to 30s. to be paid in cash. The labour of students must be satisfactory in order to be accepted as part payment for board. Economical, enterprising students rarely fail to remain in school, some of them working out as much as half of the cost of their board. The institution does not guarantee that a student will be able to work out any definite portion of the cost of his schooling. The amount earned will vary according to the value of the work done and the diligence with which the student applies himself.

With a good outfit of clothing uniform, and after providing for books, entrance fee, etc., £14 to £15 to be paid in cash for board should be sufficient to carry an industrious student through a term of nine months in the Day School.

Night School students work during the day on the farm or at some other industry and attend school for two hours at night, five nights in the week, for a year or more. In some cases Night School students are permitted to choose and work at their trade while in Night School. Such students are paid for their work according to its value. When their earnings are not sufficient to cover their board, the difference is to be paid in cash.

By putting in full time and doing satisfactory work, Night School students not pursuing a trade have an opportunity to earn the cost of their board, and what may be earned over this amount is placed to their credit in the Institute Treasury to help pay their board as they further pursue their studies. *In special cases* students are permitted to draw on their accounts, by orders, for books, clothing, etc. Agricultural students alone are permitted to receive a small proportion of their wages in cash.

DISCIPLINE.

The moral discipline of the students in view of their large number, is notably and creditably sustained. Apart from the cast-iron rules and regulations of the institute, which keep all preoccupied one way or another every minute of the day and evening, the Y.M.C.A. and other such bodies play a large part in elevating the general tone of the community. A systematic detective and constabulary force, recruited from among selected and responsible students vigilantly guard every building and every yard of the grounds day and night.

THE ACADEMIC DEPARTMENT.

Every pupil of the Institute is enrolled in the Academic Department. The student body is divided into Day School pupils and Night School pupils. The Night School pupil attends academic exercises from 6.45 to 8.30 o'clock five evenings every week. The Day School pupil attends academic exercises three days every week from 9.00 to 12.00 and from 1.30 to 4.00 o'clock. The student is thus alternately one day in school and one day at a trade.

The academic course embraces seven years' work, divided into two periods, one of three and the other of four years. The first three years are given to preparatory work. The remaining four years constitute the Normal Course proper.

Throughout the entire course there is the closest correlation between the Academic and Industrial Divisions. Much of the work on the days in which the academic studies are taken is a continuation of the work which is done in the various Industrial Divisions on the other days. This is made possible by the fact that every

35

teacher in the Academic Department visits the Industrial Divisions every week and comes in closest touch with the industrial teachers and the processes of the various trades.

The following scheme indicates the variety of subjects dealt with in the course of study for the four years of the Normal School proper,—the four years, say, after Standard V. :—

DAY SCHOOL JUNIOR CLASS (say Standard VI.) :

Reading, Grammar, Arithmetic, Concrete Geometry, Writing and Drawing, Geography, Gymnastics (for girls).

DAY SCHOOL : B. MIDDLE CLASS (say First Year Pupil Teachers).

Reading, Grammar, Arithmetic, American History, Botany (half year), Agriculture (half year), Hygiene (half year), Gymnastics (for girls).

DAY SCHOOL : A MIDDLE CLASS (say Second Year Pupil Teachers).

Required—Reading, including spelling, Grammar, Algebra ; Elective — Bookkeeping, Ancient History, Chemistry.

The students of the A Middle Class are required to take five subjects. In addition to the three definite subjects named in the required list, the student shall elect two subjects from the electives. The elective of at least one of these two subjects must be determined by the trade or vocation of the student.

DAY SCHOOL : SENIOR CLASS (say Third Year Pupil Teachers).

Required—English, including spelling ; Elective—

Education, Economics, Modern History, Bookkeeping, Geometry or Physics or Chemistry.

All students in the Senior Class are required to take four subjects. In addition to the one subject (English) named in the required list, the student shall take three other subjects from the list of electives; at least two of such subjects shall be chosen according to the demand of the student's trade or profession.

In his utterances and books, the Principal, Dr. Booker T. Washington, it seems to me at least, does not bring out the intrinsic merit of this academic department into its rightful prominence. Somewhere in the "Story of my Life" he claims, modestly I think, that the aim is rather to teach little and thoroughly, than much and insufficiently. The above list does not support this, and the scope of the following analytical description of the various subjects possibly refutes it. Indeed some prominent educators who have visited Tuskegee have in their enthusiasm delivered themselves of incredibly extravagant expressions in eulogy of this branch.

To give the details would occupy twenty pages. Suffice it here to say that the classes I reckon equal to the Cape P.T. 1, 2 and 3 seem to do far more work than those corresponding to them at the Cape can do. The subjects comprise: English Mathematics (Arithmetic, Algebra, Concrete and Plane Geometry, Elementary Civil Engineering, Bookkeeping, Free Hand Industrial Drawing, Writing); Economics (History and Geography, Industrial History); Natural Science (Chemistry, Physics, Mechanics, Heat, Electricity, Light, Sound), Hygiene, Education, Kindergarten, Music (vocal and instrumental), Public Speaking.

The above syllabus is, without doubt, based upon rigidly practical considerations. The exclusion of modern and dead languages is due, probably, rather

37

to the necessities of the heavy industrial counterpart programme than to an underestimation of their cultural value.

Admirable as this scheme may be, its success in actual working becomes wholly dependent on the calibre and energy of the teaching staff, where there are, as in Tuskegee, no regular government inspectors, nor external examiners to sift the classes.

With mediocre or indifferent teachers, possessing full power to pass, 'condition,' or fail students, it is easy to see that but for the conscientious and vigilant supervision of the Director, the standard of attainment may become highly uncertain. On the other hand this freedom gives opportunities to an enterprising Director and staff to introduce and develop their own particular principles.

The results of this have been so good at Tuskegee that some quotations from a number of the most prominent American educational authorities will be appropriate.

These are excerpts from the opinions of members of the Department of Superintendence of the National Educational Association after visiting Tuskegee :—

From Mr. W. M. Pierce (Superintendent of Public Schools, Ridgeway, Pennsylvania): "It has been my business for years to watch the work of teachers critically every day. I inspected the teaching at Tuskegee as I would have done in our own schools, and for the work of every teacher I saw I have only commendation. I have rarely seen greater earnestness or greater tact in teaching than was displayed there. Every teacher, too, seemed to have his or her aim in teaching the lesson clearly in mind, and drove straight to the point.

"One of the things that impressed me most was the real practical nature of the work of your school. In our public schools, we have been talking about correlation of

38

work, and of giving such instruction as should fit our students for real life, but when I saw the work at Tuskegee it seemed to me that you had completely solved the problem we have been talking about."

From Mr. Henry M. Maxon (City Superintendent of Schools, Plainfield, New Jersey): "I think every one of our party felt that the day spent at Tuskegee was the most valuable that we have spent anywhere for a long time. No one who has not visited Tuskegee can get any adequate conception of the work you are doing, no matter how much he may read what you have written, or however much he may listen to what you say in your lectures.

From Mr. C. P. Cary (State Superintendent, Department of Public Instruction, State of Wisconsin): "If I were to express fully my appreciation of the work I saw in passing through the institution, it would probably seem extravagant. It was, upon the whole, the best work I have ever seen in any educational institution. The instruction was the most vital and real that I ever witnessed; it was closer to realities, and there was an effort made to secure adequate and complete comprehension on the part of the students that delighted me. I have made remarks similar to the above to many people in my own State since my return. Your school has many lessons for the people of the North, the East and the West to learn. Compared with yours much of our instruction seems academic, bookish and unreal."

Special significance attaches to the statements of Mrs. Young, who is regarded as the foremost lady educational authority in the States. The Chicago *Inter-Ocean* in its issue of March 4th, 1913, reports Mrs. Ella Flagg Young, Superintendent of Schools, Chicago, Illinois, as follows: "We always have heard and thought of the work at Tuskegee as a problem of teaching an inferior race. As

39

a matter of fact, the whole problem of education is being wrestled with down there, and it is meeting with as successful solution as can be pointed to anywhere in this country. Boards of Education anywhere in the country could take pointers from the work that is being done at Tuskegee, and they would profit by them.

"I have talked with some of the biggest educational men in this country on this same subject, and they all say the same thing."

The Philadelphia *North American* in an interview also quotes her to the following effect: "Mrs. Young came to this city from Tuskegee Institute, where she has been observing methods of instruction. She declared the theory of education is better understood and practised there than in 95 per cent. of the schools of the country."

Quotations of more or less the same type may be made from at least eighty-seven other educational authorities, possessing high credentials for pronouncing an opinion on the subject, throughout the length and breadth of the States.

In considering the question of applying this syllabus to South Africa, several points have to be borne in mind which constitute important differences between the circumstances of black people in the two countries concerned.

American coloured institutions fall roughly into two groups: (a) The purely collegiate and university organizations, training for degrees and professions, and having branches for Theology, Dentistry, Pharmacy, Law, and so forth; for example: Howard University, Washington, D.C.: Wilberforce University, Georgia; Lincoln University, Pennsylvania; and medical colleges like Meharry College, Tennessee, and Shaw University, North Carolina, about a hundred in all.

(b) Agricultural, mechanical and industrial institutions,

about four hundred in all, and of which Tuskegee is the largest. The latter group aggregate about seven times as many students as are in the former.

Now in South Africa we have only one college offering ambitious and talented native youths with the degree education such as is available at the Atlanta, Wilberforce and Howard Universities for negroes.

The American negroes have always had the great Northern White University colleges open to them; in South Africa such advantages are non-existent, this fact compelling a considerable number of youths to go to America and England.

It is from these Northern colleges that the Staff for Tuskegee and other industrial schools is largely drawn. Without them, Tuskegee would, in the words of a Northern critic, "have been unthinkable," (Prof. Du Bois) and, in my opinion, impossible in its present constitution and Southern locality.

Hygiene and Book-keeping are highly necessary in curricula for South African Native Schools. Their educational and practical value is too patent to need special advocacy here.

The Bible Training School does not offer much in the way of new suggestions, for a similar course is fully carried out in connection with various denominational mission boards in South Africa.

DEPARTMENT OF MECHANICAL INDUSTRIES.

This department is conducted on an elaborate scale and with a proficiency that has made the Institute unique. Expert and experienced instructors only are requisitioned to take charge of the teaching. It includes mainly industries for young men. There are few schools which offer to young coloured men thorough instruction in these industries, and the opportunity to serve as apprentices is rapidly passing away. A rare chance is therefore offered in this department for acquiring a trade.

In arranging the course of study, four things are kept in view :

1. To inculcate the dignity of labour.
2. To teach every student a vocation.
3. To supply the demand for trained industrial leaders.
4. To assist the students in paying all or part of their expenses.

The following trades and industries are taught : Architectural and Mechanical Drawing, Blacksmithing, Woodturning, Brickmaking, Brickmasonary, Plastering and Tilesetting, Carpentry, Applied Electricity, Founding, Harnessmaking, Printing, Carriage-trimming, Steam Engineering Machine Shop Practice, Plumbing and Steamfitting, Shoemaking, Tinsmithing, Tailoring, Wheelwrighting, Bookkeeping and Accounting as applied to the trades. There are altogether forty industries taught at Tuskegee and all with remarkable efficiency for the students all make good in these in after life. The details would cover a great many pages if set out here.

There is a system of apprenticeship in Lovedale in branches like Wagon-making, Printing, Bookbinding, Shoemaking, Carpentry and so on* worked in conjunction with evening classes. The difference is that this is not optional in Tuskegee. All students are compelled to chose some trade or other. The class and the commercial value of the work produced in the divisions of Carpentry, Wheelwrighting, Repairs, Machining and Steam Engineering, are among the most astounding

*See "The South African Natives," Murray, London.

revelations of this institution from the point of view of a South African Native to whom these are mysteries reserved, largely for Europeans.

The teaching of Landscape Gardening and Home Ornamentation might be adopted in South Africa at but little expense.

BUSINESS AGENT'S DEPARTMENT.

The Business Agent's Department is charged with the duties of buyiug and selling for the Institute. He is also responsible for the conduct of the boarding department, the butchering and baking divisions. The course of study in each of these two divisions covers a period of two years.

DEPARTMENT OF WOMEN'S INDUSTRIES.

Women's industries are conducted in a commodious building, and consist of :—Plain Sewing, Dressmaking, Ladies' Tailoring, Millinery, Cooking, Laundry, Soap-making, Domestic Training of Girls, Practice Cottage, Mattressmaking, Basketry, Broom-making, Child Nursing and Nurture.

Out of many pages of detail, the following may be selected as interesting specimens :—

COOKING.

The Division of Cooking uses two kitchens, three dining rooms, a sitting room, a bed room and bath room properly fitted. Constant practice is afforded all of the young women in the care of these rooms. During the past year five hundred girls have received training in this division. The Institute insists that every girl shall receive instructions in Cooking. Special stress is laid upon cooking plain, ordinary food. The course of instruction extends over four years.

PRACTICE COTTAGE.

In order to give the girls practical demonstration in home-keeping and to develop their sense of responsibility, a five-room cottage called "Practice Cottage" is set aside, in which the Senior girls keep house. The class is divided into sections of five girls each, who live in the cottage, having entire charge of themselves and the house, doing all of the work pertaining to housekeeping, from the Monday's washing to the Saturday's preparations for Sunday. They are charged with the responsibility of purchasing the food supplies, being allowed a sufficient amount of money to cover cost of the same, including fuel and light, and are required to make accurate weekly statements of all expenditures of the home.

Sewing and Dressmaking have for a long time been taught in South Africa, but the Cooking syllabus in Tuskegee could well be copied in its entirety. Scientific cooking is the most conspicuous department in a household and certainly comes before dressing in importance. King's College, London University, has, of late years, recognized the value of culinary and domestic science training for women graduates and has made it possible for women to take a degree in these subjects.

The question is undoubtedly worthy of the attention of the white and native school teachers. At any rate in all the existing Native Schools that attempt domestic training for girls, this may be found immediately practicable. Perhaps for the supervision of the department it might be found advisable to import specialists from Tuskegee, or better still, have a chosen number of local native teachers trained by Government and equipped with the necessary apparatus as well as an inexpensive five-roomed iron structure for a Practice Cottage.

44

The object of a complete household training for girls, according to Mrs. B. T. Washington in an interview, is "to fit girls to make homes for themselves as well as for the communities to which they go. Though everything is taught in the line of Sewing and Millinery, emphasis is specially laid on Cooking and Housekeeping. The great cry among coloured communities is for girls who can cook scientifically, that is with efficiency, economy and commonsense; girls who can keep a house in proper order; keep rugs and mats in their proper places and proper sanitary condition; and girls who can see to keeping sheets, pillowcases, and table cloths always white-clean. In the Extension course the purpose is to teach the wives of farmers how to manage a home, and to inculcate ideas as well as ideals of home life. Black people everywhere in the world, I care not where, want to be taught cleanliness and neatness. These are virtues attainable only through training or inheritance; and this they either have not, or possess only in a small and negligible degree." These principles are vitalised in the Practice Cottage. Every girl student is for these reasons compelled to take the Cooking course. The course in Child Nursing and Nurture is important, and in places like Lovedale and Butterworth where there is a well equipped hospital, facilities could be made for a complete adaptation of this Tuskegee idea, for the benefit of all girl students.

THE DEPARTMENT OF AGRICULTURE.

This Department has every imaginable advantage in the way of buildings, stock grounds, fields, gardens, and other appropriate appointments. The Principal has probably shown his interest and attention more to the development of this branch, than to any other. It is as much a practical lesson to South Africa as anything else Tuskegee can offer. The question, therefore, is not whether it be adopted or no, but how best to introduce it on the model of Tuskegee.

Either a complete staff of Tuskegee graduates might be imported, as has already been done by the German Government in West Africa, and stationed, say at Lovedale, as a Government experiment; or a selected number of Bantu students be sent at Government expense to take the full course at Tuskegee, with the express purpose of working it out in South Africa.

In fact the United States Government has for more than eight years educated and supported, as is still done, about twenty native Porto Rico students at a time in Tuskegee by a system of scholarships requiring these students, on qualifying, to teach and conduct agricultural and industrial work in Porto Rico under Government auspices.

The plan has answered splendidly, I am told.

In the case of South Africa, the selection might be arranged so as to include native Farm Demonstrators of the type employed by the United States Government.

The Department of Agriculture is divided into the following divisions:

Farm crops; truck gardening; fruit growing; care and management of horses and mules; dairy husbandry; dairying; swine raising; beef production and slaughtering; canning; veterinary science and poultry raising.

The demand for men trained in these divisions has become great.

The school farm consists of 2,400 acres: 1,000 acres under cultivation. In the Farm Crops Division it is the plan to raise all foodstuffs as nearly as possible for the 1,200 head of livestock owned by the school. The young men in this division get a splendid opportunity in general farming and in the use of improved farm implements and intensive methods.

The full details would occupy many pages here.

The Two Weeks' School for farmers is possible in all schools having an Agricultural course. It is one of the means of making a school exert vital influence around its vicinity.

"It should be understood that at such institutions as Hampton Institute and ·Tuskegee Institute, industrial education is not emphasized because coloured people are to receive it, but because the ripest educational thought of the world approves it; because the undeveloped material resources of the South make it peculiarly important for both races; and because it should be given in a large measure to any race, regardless of colour, which is in the same state of development as the Negro." [" Tuskegee and its people," p. 9.]

DEPARTMENT OF RESEARCH,
CONSULTING CHEMIST AND EXPERIMENT STATION.

This Department seeks to give, in a technical and experimental way, scientific facts which will lead to a better knowledge of Agriculture in all its branches.

The laboratory work is made simple, clear and to the point. Both physical and chemical analysis of soils, fertilizers, forage plants, milk, butter, cheese, food adulterations, dietaries, etc., are given special attention.

In the Experiment Station numerous experiments are attempted in the improvement of the soil, cotton and corn breeding, inoculation of the soil, experiments with fertilizers, test of forage plants, various garden vegetables, etc.

In the poultry yard the student has an opportunity

47

to see several kinds of incubators in operation and various experiments in feeding, breeding, etc., being conducted.

The soil around Tuskegee Institute happens to be poor, agriculturally speaking. The Institute, turning this disadvantage into an advantage has shown, by experiment and research, how it can be used with profit. In this connection there is an interesting passage from " Working with the Hands," by Booker T. Washington (page 135-137), which may be quoted : "As I have said many times, it is my conviction that the great body of the Negro population must live in the future as they have done in the past, by the cultivation of the soil ; and the most hopeful service now to be done is to enable the race to follow agriculture with intelligence and diligence.

I have just finished [1904] reading a little pamphlet written by Mr. W. Carver, Director of the Agricultural Department at Tuskegee, giving the results of some of his experiments in raising sweet potatoes for one year. This coloured man has shown in plain, simple language, based on scientific principles, how he has raised two hundred and sixty-six bushels of sweet potatoes on a single acre of common land, and made a net profit of one hundred and twenty-one dollars [£24 about]. The average yield of sweet potatoes to the acre, in the part of the South where this experiment was tried, is thirty-seven bushels per acre. This coloured man is now preparing to make this same land produce five hundred bushels of potatoes.

I have watched this experiment with a great deal of pleasure. The deep interest shown by the neighbouring white farmers has been most gratifying. I do not believe that a single white farmer who visited the field to see the unusual yield, ever thought of having any prejudice or feeling against this coloured man, because his education had enabled him to make a marked success of raising sweet potatoes. There were, on the other hand, many evidences of respect for this coloured man, and of gratitude for the information which he had furnished.

If we had a hundred such coloured men in each county in the South, we could make their education felt in meeting the world's needs, there would be no race problem. But in order to get such men, those interested in the education of the Negro must begin to look facts and conditions in the face.

Too great a gap has been left between the Negro's real condition and the position for which we have tried to fit him through the medium of our text-books. We have overlooked in many cases the fact that long years of experience and discipline are necessary for any race before it can get the greatest amount of good out of text-books.

Much that the Negro has studied presupposes conditions that do not, for him, exist.

The weak point in the past has been that no attempt has been made to bridge the gap between the Negro's educated brain and his opportunity for supplying the wants of an awakened mind."

" There has been almost no thought of connecting the educated brain with the educated hand. It is almost a crime to take young men from the farm, or from farming districts, and educate them, as is too often done, in everything except agriculture, the one subject with which they should be most familiar. The result is that the young man, instead of being educated to love agriculture, is educated out of sympathy with it; and instead of returning to his father's farm after leaving college, to show him how to produce more with less labour, the young man is often tempted to go into the city or town to live by his wits."

The pithy, practical, and commonsense character of this book make me enthusiastic enough to suggest its wide circulation among white and black in South Africa. The above passage is only one among many others equally forceful. And if this report can do nothing else but bring that passage into due prominence, the writer will feel more than compensated for his Tuskegee mission.

Some society, some philanthropist, or Government might well consider a plan for placing it into the hands of all students completing the higher classes.

It is a characteristic statement of the Tuskegee Head, and in accordance with these motives every student of the B Middle class is now compelled to go through the short course in Elementary Agriculture.

"While purely literary or professional education was not opposed by the white population, it was something in which they found little or no interest, beyond a confused hope that it would result in producing a higher and better type of Negro manhood. The minute it was seen that through industrial education the Negro youth was not only studying chemistry, but also how to apply the knowledge of chemistry to the enrichment of the soil, or to cooking, or to dairying, and that the student was being taught not only geometry and physics, but their application to blacksmithing, brickmaking, farming, and what not, then there began to appear for the first time a common bond between the two races and co-operation between the North and South.

"One of the most interesting and valuable instances of that kind that I know of is presented in the case of Mr. George W. Carver, one of our instructors in agriculture at the Tuskegee Institute. For some time it has been his custom to prepare articles containing information concerning the conditions of local crops, and warning the

50

farmers against the ravages of certain insects and diseases. The local white papers are always glad to publish these articles, and they are read by white and coloured farmers.

Some months ago a white land-holder in Montgomery County asked Mr. Carver to go through his farm with him for the purpose of inspecting it. While doing so Mr. Carver discovered traces of what he thought was a valuable mineral deposit, used in making a certain kind of paint. The interest of the land-owner and the agricultural instructor at once became mutual. Specimens of the deposits were taken to the laboratories of the Tuskegee Institute and analysed by Mr. Carver. In due time the land-owner received a report of the analysis, together with a statement showing the commercial value and application of the mineral. I shall not go through the whole interesting story, except to say that a stock company composed of some of the best white people in Alabama, has been organized, and is now preparing to build a factory for the purpose of putting their product on the market. I hardly need to add that Mr. Carver has been freely consulted at every step, and his services generously recognized in the organization of the concern. When the company was being formed, a testimonial was embodied in the printed copy of the circular to George W. Carver, Director of the Department of Agriculture, Tuskegee, Alabama. (From "The Fruits of Industrial Training." By Booker T. Washington, in the "Atlantic Monthly, November, 1903)."

Other branches of this department are: The Local Conferences; The Farmers' Institute; The Short Course of Agriculture to neighbouring farmers for two weeks yearly; Farm Demonstration Work; Mothers' Meetings The Ministers' Association; The Town Night School.

The practical effects of the Extension Department are

51

considered, by the Principal, to be as far-reaching as, if not more than, those of the actual school work. Anyway there is no gainsaying their value to the immediate vicinity of the institution. The general aim of the department has been (1) to change public opinion and turn the attention of the people in directions where there was hope for them. This has been the work of the Negro Conference and various agencies that have grown up to help to complete its work; (2) to educate the people on the soil, encourage better methods of farming and so induce Negro farmers' children to remain on the soil. This has been the work of the Farmers' Institute, the Demonstration Farming and the Jesup Agricultural Wagon.

It has been estimated that the Extension work yearly reaches at least a hundred thousand people, outside the students; and that it is owing largely to its influence that Negro property in Macon County has, during the last twenty years, increased by 600 per cent.

The Annual Negro Conference was started in February, 1891. In that year Principal Booker T. Washington sent out invitations to about seventy-five representative Negroes in Macon County, farmers, mechanics, school teachers and ministers. The majority of the men who came to the conference were farmers. Instead of seventy-five, something like four hundred responded to this invitation. The success of the first conference has been repeated each year since, and the fame of its annual meetings has extended until Negro farmers come from all over the South to attend them.

A Conference Agent is employed by the school whose duty is to organise local conferences in different communities in the State and visit those conferences already established in order to encourage them in the work. At the last accounting 105 local organizations had been established.

A graphic account of these conferences was given some time ago, in "The Voice of the Negro," by Mr. Emmett J. Scott, the Institute Secretary, who apart from shrewd business and diplomotic qualities, (for he has acted as a United States Government Commissioner to Liberia) possesses brilliant literary attainments.

Space forbids a quotation of more than one or two sentences from that article: " Eighty-five per cent. of the Negro people of the South live on plantations and farms and in the country districts. How to stimulate this all-too-inert mass, how to get at it, and quicken the necessary following without which leaders lead a forlorn hope —that were a question and a task. But these Conferences do it. They bring together annually men and women who are down and who know they are down, but desire to get up. Also they bring together educated men and women, white and black, interested in these first named, and together they confer. The point of acutest need is developed and remedies suggested; how some man or woman has succeeded is the token by which others may succeed. Influence and example wield their sceptre where froth and declamation backed not by tangible achievement, would fail; and so example has a large place in the proceedings. Then, again, the Conferences are devoted not to abstractions, but to concrete problems, and what is most important, the solution of these problems."

"As for the farmers and their wives, they unhesitatingly declare their faith in the efficacy of these Conferences; though unschooled, they possess an inborn eloquence that comes to the surface on this, their 'one day in school,' that cannot fail to convince all that heartily grateful are they for the chance to come once a year to the Tuskegee Mecca for a new baptism ot thrift, industry and the kindred virtues of sober, contented and decent living."

One chapter, and one of the best, in "Working with the Hands," is devoted to the history of Mrs. B. T. Washington's organization work and her Tuskegee town coloured "Mothers' Meetings." The latter have now extended their influence to small communities in other parts of the State and beyond to other portions of the country.

More than twenty of such districts in Macon County and elsewhere maintain meetings of this kind.

About two thousand women on the farms are reached through the medium of these meetings.

The Farm Demonstration Work is possibly the one branch which can be adopted with least difficulty by the South African Government; because it is in vogue throughout the States and its application could be made with the consultation of some of the United States Government agricultural experts.

From the Report of the United States Commissioner, I select two examples of the Demonstration work among Negroes:

In 1912 there were 32 Negro Farm Demonstrators. In speaking of the work of these agents, Mr. Bradford Knapp said, in his report to the General Education Board: 'I believe that it is safe to say that these, together with the negro farmers and tenants who are receiving direct instruction through white agents, will bring the total of negroes being instructed up to about 20,000!'

As an illustration of the work of the negro demonstrations, Mr. Knapp describes the activities of one of them in the Wellville community in Virginia: 'The improvement in the Wellville community under the special superintendence of J. B. Pierce, is a source of great interest and presents a showing that is little short of remarkable. Some of these negro farmers are making yields of corn from 50 to 200 per cent. larger than they did formerly, and are doing it at less cost per bushel.

GENERAL REMARKS ON THE SYLLABUS.

(a) Tuskegee students are paid for their labour on a graduated scale and by the day. They keep cards in which their instructors note the time spent and the value of the work done. These are sent to the office where bills are made up ; and if the work done yield value exceeding the dues, then the money is placed to the credit of the student. But if the difference be against the student, then it has to be paid in cash ; and if the debt remain unsettled for longer than a month, the student is suspended from academic classes until sufficient work is done to meet the adverse balance.

Students keep their money at the Institute Savings Bank, and it is fascinating to watch them at the Bank office, carrying on their banking transactions like London commercial men, signing cheques, withdrawing or making deposits from their labour earnings. To them, the Institute is no mere model but a living business centre where every man stands or falls by his work and keenness. They are thus taught, as is done in no South African school, to do work of a definite and calculable commercial value to the school, proportion-ately earn money, bank it and dispense it like business men.

Indeed, the senior and post graduate students, especially in the Agricultural Department, not only pay for their education outright in this way but actually accumulate savings of their own.

The school therefore inculcates upon the boys and girls, in a practical manner, the idea of preparing to go out into a world of work, of work with the hands, and of looking forward to that world. They learn mathematics and grammar not with the purpose of shirking and escaping manual labour but so that these may come to their aid as weapons in a life struggle. Large

55

numbers of them find it the most natural thing to spend the Summer Vacation in trade employment, amassing money.

(b) A remarkable phenomenon about Tuskegee is that there is sufficient structural work in the plant regularly to provide labour enough for all students. It is doubtful if this can be said of any other institution. The expansion has reached such proportions that there is an ever increasing and continuous demand for elementary and rudimentary work of every sort keeping employment certain. This point is vividly worked out by Arthur M. Evans in "Working out the Race Problem," in a passage which runs as follows :

" Three or four years ago the University of Cincinnati started to educate the students in its technical courses by providing alternate days for theory and practice, one day being spent in the class room and the next day in a real factory, where the students would not only learn how to build things, but would have the inspiration coming from the building of things actually to be used. This idea created a furore in the educational world : it was acclaimed as the newest and the most advanced idea in technical education. Booker Washington, however, has been applying that idea at Tuskegee for the last thirty years. The students spend one day in the class room, and one day on the farm or in the shops, where they turn out products that are to be used.

The great cry among the great technical colleges has been that in the practice work the students build things that are torn down as soon as they are constructed. The energizing force that comes from creating something that is to be utilized is lacking. What inspiration is there in building a model bridge when the student knows it is to be torn down as soon as the last bolt is in place ? Educators in technical institutions have lamented this loudly.

56

At Tuskegee the boy in the tailor shop makes uniforms that are worn by the students. The head of the department still talks of the suit of clothes the boys made for Andrew Carnegie for £3, which the ironmaster pronounced as fine a fit as he had ever worn. In the harness and saddleryshop the boys manufacture things that are not torn to pieces as soon as they are finished. The head of the shop speaks proudly of the £60 double harness which the boys made for Colonel Roosevelt. In the wagonshop, the smithy, the broom-shop, the brick yard, the canning factory, the foundry, the mattress-shop, the shoemaking-shop, the printing office, the tinsmithing-shop, in all the forty different trades and industries, the boys are not only getting an occupational education, but they are deriving the inspiration that comes from making something to be used. At Tuskegee it is deemed as important to turn out inspired cobblers and plumbers as inspired architects and landscape artists.

(c) The method of employing students instead of professional labour is without doubt expensive. For example the present Dining Hall building, estimated to cost £34,000, eventually cost £45,000 on account of the alterations and mistakes that are inevitable in the process of masonic instruction.

On the contrary when it is reckoned that all this money went directly into the pockets of the students and in the cost of providing practice, it is easy to prove that this was the cheapest device for combining instruction with Institute expansion, consistently with practical results. And Tuskegee has been courageous enough to follow this method with almost all the school buildings, now numbering well over a hundred.

This scheme is applied to other industries too.

(d) The practicability of dovetailing industrial with academic education, is thus convincing. In this connection it may be well to call to mind that the

57

Slavery Emancipation of 1865 has had unique results in America. In West Indies it was given only after several years' of apprenticeship, during which time the slaves were consciously and suitably trained to prepare to support themselves for the approaching time of liberation. This is claimed to account for the satisfactory racial relations in those islands. In America the slaves were all unleashed into liberty with a suddenness that has proved harmful both to the owners and the freed.

The sudden and enforced material loss engendered a bitter resentment in the hearts of many owners.

The slaves were so helpless that some actually chose to remain with their former masters! Others developed a disdain for manual labour and committed mistakes. They did not understand that they were freed from being worked and not from working. Courses of education were philanthropically and otherwise devised, that had little relation to the immediate needs. It fell to the lot of Booker Washington, inspired by Hampton Institute methods, to possess both the psychological foresight and devoted courage to fabricate, in Tuskegee, an educational machine that fitted in with the circumstances.

The needs, the immediate needs, of the masses, became, in effect, the Tuskegee motto.

Not satisfied with mere generalities, the school, on its own initiative, carries out its principles in the town of Tuskegee itself by means of the Extension work, in the neighbourhood of the five mile radius, in its county of Macon, and in the whole State of Alabama.

(e) Statistics of the work of Tuskegee graduates go to show that the flourishing condition of Negro agriculture in Macon County is due to Tuskegee; and this influence is felt to a greater or less degree throughout the South. These results are justly claimed by the training in agriculture and industries on the basis of what has been called Correlation.* We have seen that Correlation, though almost a by-word in theoretical pedagogy, has had to wait for the Hampton and Tuskegee founders to receive a practical application.

It is evident that the choice of teachers requires supreme judgment because they, too, require to be "broken in" into the Tuskegee idea. Their work demands more energy, personal devotion and, indeed, self-denial, than that of the average teacher, to carry out the programme in its ideal form.

For these reasons it would seem that an experimental application of this curriculum in two or three willing institutions in South Africa could with Government support for necessary additions in the staff and working machinery prove practicable.

In South Africa there is room, yea, urgency, for the development of present institutions in such a way that they provide education which will (1) like Tuskegee deal with the immediate needs of the majority and masses of the black races, and (2) like Howard University, enable native teachers to qualify themselves for administering it.

RECOMMENDATIONS.

An attempt has been made here to provide a reference list to the suggestions made.

1. Substitutes for Military Training (page 33).
2. Landscape Gardening and Home Ornamentation recommended (page 43).
3. The Extension in South African Schools of Hygiene and Bookkeeping (page 41).
4. Cooking and Housekeeping (page 43), and Child Nurture (page 44).

---

* For considerations of space an excellent paper on "Correlation at Tuskegee" by J. T. Williamson, B.SC., is omitted at this point

5. Dissemination of Washington's book "Working with the Hands" (page 50).
6. The Governmental training of Natives in agriculture.
7. Agricultural Students (page 46, 54); Native Rural Supervisors.
8. Native Farm Demonstrators (page 54).
9. Ampler provision for Native Higher Education (page 59).
10. The payment system in Industrial Schools (page 55, 56, 57).

GENERAL IMPRESSIONS OF TUSKEGEE.

The village of Tuskegee is in the heart of Alabama, in the Southern States, forty-four miles from the Capital town Montgomery, and 1015 miles from New York by the Pennsylvania, Southern Alabama and West Point and Tuskegee Railways.

Though far from any large town it is easy of access the railroad reaching the grounds of the Institute.

It is in what is called the Black Belt, that is, where the Negro population predominates, and in one of the most picturesque districts of the Macon County.

Among the things that impressed me most on reaching Tuskegee were the magnificent buildings. The Dining Hall is a masonic triumph and outcome of Negro design. Its plan is boldly original, its aspect picturesque, even fanciful, and its objects have been more than successfully served. Facing it is the majestic White Memorial Building, dormitory for girls. The imposing Carnegie Library crowns the quadrangle formed by these and subsidiary structures. The Academic Building, called the Collis P. Huntingdon Memorial Building, is not as beautiful and solid as the quartz rock Education Building at Lovedale but is larger and more labyrin-

60

thine in scheme. A rough idea of the gigantic proportions of the plant may be made from the fact that apart from the above named, there are nearly ten other buildings which are only less impressive than these, and about a hundred others, the property of the Institution, to say nothing of the extent of 2,345 acres of land.

The absence of white men, the successful administration of a purely Negro faculty, in an intellectual village of this sort is not among the least significant phenomena of Tuskegee. The business discipline in evidence everywhere, to minutest detail, is almost wonderful. Hired labour is practically nil. It is the students who act as office boys, attend to the dormitories, act as engine foremen and the fire brigade, run the electric plant and steam pump room, sweep the avenues, water and mow the lawns, act as white-capped waitresses at the dining halls; it is they who are the railway luggage porters, Post Office and Express Service men, milkmen, garden and farm-hands; most miraculous to tell, they engage in these and every kind of menial work without loss of dignity, without feeling socially inferior to anyone else. The boy who comes with oily clothes and begrimed hands from the machine room is soon washed and gets into his clean clothes at the sound of the dinner bell, to shake hands with you and meet his fellows on terms of mutual respect.

The staff of the Institute is carefully and admirably selected. The men in power seem to understand, and what is more important, to be able to interpret the ideas, aims, and the temper of the Principal to a perfect degree. Lastly, there are fundamental conditions in American Negro life which form noticeable differences to those of the Bantu.

(1) The Slavery Emancipation produced a social and political revolution among the 4,000,000 who were suddenly and dramatically thrown loose from bondage.

The consequence was that there arose a pressing necessity for organizations of all kinds to keep order. For generations a bold and brainy leader has been necessary to lead the Negro, who in his turn was always willing, even eager, to be led. The number of Negro organizations is amazing, particularly the secret societies. Now the Bantu have been practically free from such a political upheaval. Their traditional moral codes, their regard for family life, their ideals of discipline under the tribal system, notwithstanding that labour-life and town influences have tended to deterioration, have remained undisturbed, notably in Basutoland and in the Transkei. On the contrary, slavery instilled a habit of industry, into the development of the South. Indeed, in the South the Negro need not seek labour, it has been said, but labour seeks him. The expansion of trade, rail road highways and land cultivation proffer him continuous opportunities.

(2) The American Negroes have been able to count largely upon the generosity of white citizens for their institutions. While Tuskegee has to raise £30,000 yearly from the public, it has taken a decade to raise half that sum for the South African Native College. And although the Scotch and English Churches and funds from the missionary bodies have been responsible for Lovedale, Healdtown, Morija, and so forth, they cannot be compared to the liberality of those Americans who have felt it their duty to educate the Negro.

(3) Nearly half of the American Negroes are enrolled as Church communicants. The number of those who do not attend, or come under the direct influences of religions and Churches is small. Indeed from my observation, the American Negro seems to feel it the most natural thing to go to Church whatever be the immediate motive. This religions nature has resulted in the

62

establishment of countless churches and schools. The population is 10,000,000; they have 40,000 churches, and 4,300,000 communicants. These figures and others on philanthropy and missionary propaganda cannot be paralleled in South Africa.

The percentage of Negro illiteracy in America has dwindled at this rate: 1863, 95%; 1873, 79%; 1883, 70%; 1893, 57%; 1903, 44%; 1913, 30%.

(4) In contrast to the implicit and slavish trust in ancestral customs resulting, among the Bantu, in inertia and apathy toward the white man's civilization, the American Negro, torn from his African tribal trammels, has a hearty readiness to take up any and all new methods of business and education. This is exemplified by movements like the Negro Business Leagues, Women's Clubs, State, National, and Educational Associations and Conventions, Religious and Fraternal organizations of every description.

(5) The accident of having English as a mother tongue in an English speaking country, must mean a great deal to the American Negro.

All these circumstances are relevant and have a direct bearing upon Tuskegee; but however full be a description of Tuskegee, it cannot adequately convey the impression made by an actual visit to the spot.

BOOKER T. WASHINGTON.—A CHARACTER SKETCH.

The limited character of my acquaintance with the Principal of Tuskegee has not deterred me from attempting a little, certainly incomplete, sketch of his personality and influence; these, though almost platitudes in America, may be fresh to some in South Africa. The life of Booker T. Washington cannot be written, says J. L. M. Curry, the famous South educationist. "Incidents of birth, parentage, schooling, early

63

struggles, later triumphs, may be detailed with accuracy, but the life has been so incorporated, transfused, into such a multitude of other lives,—broadening views, exalting ideals, moulding character,—that no human being can know its deep and beneficent influence, and no pen can describe it."

His personality like that of other illustratious figures eludes analysis. It is esoteric. He is best known by his achievements, by his oratory, and by his publications, all of which are nearly synonymous with his Tuskegee work. In person, his firm and massive lips bespeak unconquerable determination; his sinewy neck, strength and doggedness; his bull-like eyes, piercing penetration. An inflexible earnestness of purpose, overcoming all obstacles, has galvanized his career. Fundamentally he believed in his work, and believed it to be worthy beyond estimation. All his interests have been subordinated to this belief, not in a philanthropic way but as a bounden duty of life. He set out to do something; and he has always remained constructive. From friend and foe he has learnt, and has always been willing to learn. Far from devoting much of his time to retaliation he has used adverse criticism for bettering himself and his work.

Profound has been the lesson impressed on him by General Armstrong, the late Hampton Institution Principal, who " was never heard to utter a single bitter word against the Southern white man notwithstanding that he had fought against him in the war." Booker Washington is more than magnanimous in his love for the Southern White man; he possesses the large and rare virtue of loving those regarded as one's enemies.

He lives in a world of realities, often stern realities, not one of dreams, idealisms, or vague impalpable abstractions. Like Lloyd George he has a personal and direct attitude, not an impersonal and detached one, toward men and things,—an attitude that preserves him from faulty generalizations about these. For example his books—with the exemption of "The Life of Frederick Douglass"—teem with the use of the first personal pronoun: "I believe I am safe when I say that I.".........; and the conclusions from his observations rarely fail him. Hence his reliable perspective of things and conditions. Early in life he understood more clearly than others that there was a genuine, nay, pathetic, desire on the part of his countrymen for education, for civilized conveniences and machinery With his knowledge of their needs he sought to furnish these, and has done so with subtle diplomacy. The Negroes have again and again, and in multifarious ways shown their appreciation of his service and its tangible nature. He has taught them what it is necessary to know ; he has taught them the dignity of labour and the importance of material development. Indeed so much stress has he laid on the acquisition of chickens and pigs, bank accounts and property, that he has lent himself to the misinterpretation of being materialistic and, if not irreligious, morally indifferent to the claims of religious propaganda. No greater mistake was ever made. He is as religious as a man can be ; and his regard for the Bible and its meaning to man's life is fully given in "Up From Slavery." To him it has been a real guide. On the other hand it may be possible to misconstrue some of his statements on this subject. And many religious ministers have not been satisfied with his attitude.

The explanation of his enjoining clergymen to preach more on the tangible things of the present life, and less on the future bliss of heaven is that he wants them to devise a correlation between religious ideals and practical life. Because it is difficult, he has said, for a hungry man to be religious and good.

As a leader he is admitted to be the most influential Negro anywhere. In the Southern States he is certainly unrivalled and is the right man in the peculiar conditions that obtain there. In the North, however, the unanimity is less complete. The social problems there are different; and the questions which agitate the more advanced coloured people are not capable of being magically settled by the gospel of work and money alone. A number of Negroes like Kelly Miller, * W. E. B. Du Bois,** feel that he does not represent their particular positions and that his politics are too compromising and harmful for their Northern circumstances, unreservedly as they admire his philosophy and achievement for the masses. The fact is that Mr. Washington really stands outside the conflicts of the political arena. He speaks on political matters and refers to them only in so far as they touch his mission and a few outstanding general questions like lynching and "Jim Crowing." So that from the circumstances of the case, men of purely political pursuits can hardly look for his active guidance and concentration. With this exception his leadership is undisputed.

So far as oratory is concerned he is the most conspicuous Negro in and outside the States. Whether he is actually the most eloquent it is not easy to judge. But if results alone be made the criterion—and here merely academic rhetoric is discounted—then he has no peer among coloured people ever since the days of Frederick Douglass. Some of his most notable speeches,

---

* Prof. of Mathematics in the Howard University.

** One of the only ten American negroes who have gained the final degree of Ph. D. at one (Harvard University) or other of the foremost American Universities.

like the epoch-making Altanta Exposition Address, are recorded in his books and elsewhere, but the great bulk are not fully published. Some of his important writings, like "Is the Negro Having a Fair Chance?" perhaps his masterpiece, appear as magazine contributions and pamphlets. [Since this sketch was written in 1913, Washington died in 1916 and his life and work have been done by Dr. Scott and Stowe in an excellent book, "Booker T. Washington, Builder of a Civilisation."]

The books are as follows:—

1. *The Future of the American Negro* (1899), which forms the best summary, perhaps, of his views on Industrial Education. Indeed the appeal for tangible aims in education becomes emotional and impassioned. That he is qualified to speak on the subject there can be no doubt. "For years I have had something of an opportunity to study the Negro at first hand; and I feel that I know him pretty well,—him and his needs, his failures and his successes, his desires and the likelihood of their fulfilment. I have studied him and his relations with his white neighbours, and striven to find how these relations may be made more conducive to the general peace and welfare both of the South and of the country at large." (p. 16).

"It seems to me that there never was a time in the history of the country when those interested in education should the more earnestly consider to what extent the mere acquiring of the ability to read and write, the mere acquisition of a knowledge of literature and science, makes men producers, lovers of labour, independent, honest, unselfish, and, above all, good. Call education by what name you please, if it fails to bring about these results among the masses, it falls short of its highest end. The science, the art, the literature, that fails to reach down and bring the humblest up to the enjoyment

67

of the fullest blessings of our government, is weak, no matter how costly the buildings or apparatus used, or how modern the methods of instruction employed. The study of arithmetic that does not result in making men conscientious in receiving and counting the ballots [votes] of their fellow men is faulty. The study of art that does not result in making the strong less willing to oppress the weak means little. How I wish that from the most cultured and highly endowed university in the Great North to the humblest log cabin school-house in Alabama, we could burn, as it were, into the hearts and heads of all, that usefulness, that service to our brother, is the supreme end of education." (pp. 18-19).

2. *Up from Slavery* (1900) has been called a "a better Uncle Tom's Cabin," for its optimism. It is as thrilling a romance of actual life as a realistic novel, and it appeals by its uncoloured, natural, and plain style. It is the most widely known of the author's books, and contains the genesis of the Tuskegee Institute.

3. *The Story of my Life* (1901) is a re-arrangement of "Up from Slavery," with copious additions like the account of the degree day at the Harvard University when Mr. Washington was recognised with an Honorary Degree of LL.D.

4. *Character Building* (1902) is a volume of selected sermonettes which Mr. Washington had been in the custom of giving to the students on Sunday evenings ever since the inception of the school. They are couched in homely, familiar, and conversational language with the frankness and benignant severity of a father speaking to his children. It is impossible to calculate the good they have been to the listeners, this being freely confessed by the writers in "Tuskegee and its People." The personal note and moral sincerity produce a tone that renders this the most charming of the series of books.

5. *Working with the Hands* (1904) is in some ways a refutation to the charges that the author preached labour education to the neglect, if not exclusion, of higher education. The principles of industrial education are, after " The Future of the American Negro," further developed, rendering this volume superlatively educative.

6. *Tuskegee and its People* (1905) is a collaboration of the Principal with several writers, including Emmett J. Scott (Secretary), and Warren Logan (Treasurer), who have sketched out the scope of the Institute. The contributions are supplemented by a compendium of brief autobiographies by some of the successful people trained at Tuskegee. This book, on account of the variety of authorship, is extremely interesting, and even entertaining.

7. *The Negro in Business* (1907) is a singular record of the energy and patience of men who have acquired material wealth starting from poverty and, often, indebtedness. Although this book is monotonous to an outsider, from a literary point of view (for its inartistic succession of biographies), it is a living thing to those who know the Negro conditions in the States, and it is more than a convenient and profitable reference guide to American natives. It serves among other things, to illustrate the commercial value to a country of the industrial activity of every section of the population.

8. *The Life of Frederick Douglass* (1907), is strikingly unlike the other books, preceding and following, on account of its lofty and grandiose literary style. As a biography it is alive, racy, adequate and fascinating, for its size.

9, 10. *The Story of the American Negro* (1909), occupies two volumes. The literary aim has been rather to encourage and inspire the Negro everywhere than to accomplish historical uniformity and completeness. The first volume has much romantic thrill, pain and joy.

The second deals with the modern Negro, and its interest is largely statistical.

11. *My Larger Education* (1911), practically continues the author's autobiography. It shows how his working theories 'and conclusions have been mathematically reached from his direct observation of men and things (especially the Denmark chapter), and not from second hand knowledge.

12. *The Man Farthest Down* (1912), is at once as fresh as a novel and solid as a Civic Report, in its treatment of the conditions of the lower classes in Europe. The differences between American and European conditions are carefully worked out so as vividly to bring out the facts of the favourable lot of the Southern Negro, by comparison, and his great opportunities despite his social asperities and political disadvantages,—opportunities which, on account of the lack of this comparative outlook, the Negro himself does not realise.

THE NATIVE TEACHER OUT OF SCHOOL.

FOREWORD.

Of the addresses delivered at the Natal Native Teachers' Conference, July, 1918, that by Mr. D. D. T. Jabavu of the South African Native College aroused the greatest interest among the large and representative audience. This was probably due first to the fact that Mr. Jabavu is himself a Native, and secondly to the familiarity of the audience with the situations dealt with. Mr. Jabavu spoke with Cape conditions in his mind, but very similar conditions exist in Natal and other parts of South Africa. Too often an environment of indifference, sloth, intemperance and worse overcomes the young teacher ; a promising career is shattered and

another name added to our already far too extensive
"black list." For the most part the deterioration in
character results from the absence of interest outside
school, for even teachers are not exempt from the operation of the rule that Satan finds mischief for idle hands
to do. In the hope that this address may serve the
double purpose of a warning and a guide it has been
printed and circulated by the Natal Provincial Administration among the Native Teachers of Natal.

C. T. LORAM,

Chief Inspector of Native Education, Natal.

Mr. Chairman, Ladies and Gentlemen,—

When I had the privilege of addressing you three
years ago at Ladysmith, I spoke on "Educational
Psychology," and endeavoured to show you how and
why you should aim at establishing a relationship
between yourselves and your pupils which should be of
the best, truest and most profitable kind, as a result of a
study of the instincts, sentiments, emotions, ways, habits,
of the children under your care. Like other lecturers, I
propose on this occasion to link up my last talk with
to-day's—that on "The Native Teacher and the Village,"
—a title which is intended to cover the relation of the
teacher to his village, location, town, Native community,
parents of pupils, and the Church (in the widest sense of
the term "Church").

In such conferences we frequently listen to oratorical
speeches that idealise and idolise the profession of
teaching as the noblest on earth, from European speakers
who have never realised from first-hand acquaintance the
actual difficulties of a native teacher's surroundings.
Let us consider a few of the difficulties most common to
Native teachers in this Province, for I presume that the
conditions I have met in the Cape are much the same as
those of Natal, and I shall assume that, as they hold good
down at the Cape Province, they are true in your case too.

Firstly, there is loneliness, for the teacher is often the best educated, and indeed the only educated person in our Native areas and locations, surrounded by an ignorant and squalid population; secondly, the want of suitable companions, for most young men and women in our villages are not edifying companions for teachers; thirdly, beer-drinking, or the alcohol demon, to which many male teachers, I regret to state, have succumbed; fourthly, impurity or immorality which, among town and town-adjoining habitations is much more rampant than is generally known; fifthly, the want of interest in studies, lack of aim, lack of aspiration or ambition to obtain higher teaching qualifications by means of further studies; sixthly, the lack of uplifting literature for reading; seventhly, the need of a study or private room; eighthly, the lack of occupation, exercise or healthy hobbies wherewith to while away the time outside school hours, for the available form of bodily exercise—that of gardening or using the hands and wielding the axe, spade, pick, saw, hammer for the thousand and one little things constantly wanting doing around one's dwelling is despised as "manual labour," beneath a teacher's dignity; ninthly, the sting of want, hunger and despair due to the absurdly small salaries that are still reckoned as good enough for a Native teacher

There are indeed other incidental troubles haunting the Native teacher in the village, but these I have just recited are painfully real ones in all conscience, and they are hardly discussed in Teachers' conferences, where these teachers are generally lectured upon the ideals of Christian life, and Froebel, and Montessori, and the Zulu language, and music and so on—anything on earth but the grim hardships of life in Native areas. Yet worries have to be faced, fought, and overcome by our teachers if we as an African race are to attain to the intellectual and moral requirements of true civilisation. And in the

72

knowledge that this is so I venture to make the following suggestions:

1. *Loneliness.* Loneliness is largely due to the fact that the teacher is too apt to work as an isolated unit, and to have no corporate feeling as a member of a large organisation to which he may look for inspiration and solace. If you teachers would join some efficient Association, say the Teachers' Christian Association, which is meant for all Native teachers in South Africa, then you will probably obtain literature that will dispel much, if not all, of this sense of isolation; and you will have yearly or other meetings to look forward to, the very anticipation of which will spell life to the teachers in remote solitudes.

2. *Companions.* As for companions one cannot make them but has to choose from one's neighbourhood, and sometimes there is not much material for choice. From my personal experience, a hard experience, I may tell you that it pays best to have no companions at all when only those of the wrong sort are at hand. You are better off without them, unless you can secure those that, having the same aims in life as you, will bring you helpful and uplifting comradeship. Of course I do not mean that you should be proud and distain to speak to other people. Nothing is further from my mind. Do by all means speak to people, but use judgment, be careful of those whom you select as regular and permanent friends, lest they drag you down to the mire, by their talk and suggestions.

3. *Intemperance.* The curse of beer-drinking and the white man's alcohol are the greatest causes of physical and moral ruination to South African Natives; and I am grieved to affirm that there are teachers in our elementary schools and even in training institutions who, behind the scenes and unknown to their authorities, have made a secret compact with the Devil of Drink. This is

indeed deplorable. I have been informed that here in Natal too there is a large percentage of teachers who "drink." If there be any present amongst you—let me trust there is not a single one—however, if perchance there be any here whose minds are not made up on the subject I pray that you will decide from this very minute, this evening, to give up alcoholic drinks unreservedly. Read that most convincing and scientific volume on the subject "Alcohol and the Human Body," by Sir Victor Horsley, M.B., B.S. (Lond.), M.D., F.R.C.S., and Miss Mary D. Sturge, M.D. (Lond.), published at 1s. by Mac-Millan and Co , London. I could talk to you a very long time on that book which graphically pictures and analyses the harmful effects that alcohol even in its smallest doses inflicts on the human body; but I hope that this passing reference to it will move you to order it and read it, and lead you to abandon drink for ever and ever. Let us therefore have a brotherhood and sisterhood of sober teachers. Have nothing to do with drinkers and drinking canteens. Even the Municipal Beer House is not a fit place for Native teachers.

4. *Impurity.* The evil of immorality or impurity is not a pleasant subject to dilate upon. It has swallowed up many of our promising teachers, male and female. In this connection one may observe that the Native has yet to make a success, if ever he will, of what is called town life, morally speaking; for instance the average Native girl who works as kitchen servant in town is lodged in backyard quarters that would demoralise a saint, for she is turned loose from the restraint of parental control, having now no responsible guardian. This is the sorriest stage of our transition from the old tribal system to the European idea of city life. In Native locations in towns, this evil is particularly rabid, and teachers who live in such localities need special grace to be saved therefrom since it is so much part of their environment. If possible,

74

and it generally is possible, avoid the company of those tainted with it, cultivate healthy-mindedness, healthy counter-activity, and the society of the pure. Read the book called "Talks to Teachers on Psychology and to Students on some of Life's Ideals," by Prof. William James, (Longmans, Green and Co.). It will be five shillings well spent. (Probably it will be in your Teachers Circulating Library). A life of regular physical exercise in the fresh air, constant employment in pure thinking, pure reading, among pure people, is more than half the battle won, say those who are well qualified to speak on this. A surer way I believe is sincerity in Christianity. Read John Bunyan's "Pilgrim's Progress" (or "Umhambo lwesi Hambi" in its Zulu translation), read it continually and again and again, like your Bible, and follow the methods by which John Bunyan overcame this sin and all other temptation.

5. *Study.* Again our teachers engage in no studies for their own advancement. Down in the Cape Province when I enter the house or hut of the ordinary teacher I expect to see no book except the old set of School management manuals with which the teacher passed his P. T. 3, (familiarly called the "Third Year"), and perhaps a Xosa Bible, and then the class books of his children and their exercise books. That is the sum total of his library. With him there is no sign of any desire to learn more, for teaching is merely a job to him. He is dead to all study. On this account a rather humorous friend of mine has called the Third Year, the "Dead Year," perhaps not without reason. Now in civilised communities the teacher lives and dies a student, for *Docere est discere.* If you teachers aspire to real civilisation you must first learn to become students for all your life; do not rest content with your present Second or First Grade. Get into the habit of Private Study, and if

75

you mean business you will not fail to find out some one in the big towns like Maritzburg and Durban to coach you up even by Correspondence, when all other resources fail you. There are other branches of study which are your exclusive privilege. For example, we want a history book on the Zulu nation, written by a pure Zulu Native, from the standpoint of Zulus, and based upon information gotten from the Zulus who remember the stories of their own people from the lips of their predecessors themselves. Present books on the subject are from the pens of Europeans who, biassed on the side of their own people in these things, too often present the Native at a disadvantage. Why should we be told so often of these "cattle-stealing savages wantonly attacking unoffending white farmers"? Surely you Zulus have some explanation of your own for all this, and there must be another side to the question. These books do not provide attractive reading for our youths for they instinctively feel that the Native in the story is being unnecessarily painted in the blackest of colours. Your Native fables, ballads, poetry, proverbs (say, on the lines of "Sechuana Proverbs" by Mr. Solomon T. Plaatje), customs, superstitions, etc., are there for you to reduce into writing ; and they can be faithfully recorded by you and by you only.

6. *Newspaper Reading.* With regard to lack of reading matter, it is a ghastly fact that eight out of ten Native teachers do not read daily papers or any other journals, being quite satisfied, like illiterate folks, to glean their information and current news and events from vague rumours and village gossip. Is this indifference to reading due to the curricula obtaining in training institutions? Are you satisfied to live, like cattle, and care not how the other half of the world lives? In England I used to see (and this was quite an ordinary

76

thing) even the poorest mine-labourer or road scavenger buy his daily half-penny newspaper to get the news fresh for himself and to keep in touch with the world of intelligence. You as teachers should each subscribe to at least two newspapers, say one English, the other, Zulu. If the expense is high then club together in groups of three or six and combine to pay, say, four shillings each a quarter or less and get your papers regularly, to ventilate your minds with the fresh breezes of new ideas from the world of science and literature.

7. *Privacy.* You need a room that you can regard as private to yourself for meditation and reading. Many teachers board and lodge in a one-roomed house or hut along with a man and his wife and five or more children, separated from this family only by a thin clumsy curtain —a morally degrading condition of things—where one cannot possibly procure quiet for private reading or study, much less for prayers. Realising, as I hope you do the need for such a room, you should begin now and set about adding a new room to your abode which will be sacred to yourself for undisturbed thinking and where you will not be interrupted by intruders. Move heaven and earth to get this. If your authorities, or manager, or inspector, or committee all fail you, then take off your coat and get some of your friends in the village to assist you to put up the required room with your own hands. Determination works miracles. And heaven helps those who help themselves.

8. *Manual Work.* Concerning the lack of manual occupation remember that the Devil always has work for idle hands to do. These are commonplace expressions but I happen to know that you do not put them into practice in your daily life. Now as a relaxation to the constant sitting and headwork of your schoolroom, I would strongly urge you to cultivate some outdoor hobby.

77

Play tennis and indulge in long-distance walks. Be familiar with the hammer and mend the broken windows, chairs- and desks of your schoolroom; put up new shelves in your kitchen, construct box chairs and small tables and little lockable bins; get your spade and dig holes for putting in young trees to decorate the approach to your home; straighten your crooked wire fences with your own hands; level the paths and roads leading to your dwelling, scour your yards and trench a portion of them for gardening purposes so as to plant beans, potatoes, peas, cabbages, etc., and enjoy as I do, the pleasure and pride of eating home grown vegetables; build a new pig-sty and raise pigs for they fetch good money now; chop your wood; do not be too proud to touch any thing in your yard during your spare time. Manual labour is NOT beneath your dignity. At our college, if I may be allowed to be personal, I shrink from nothing that I send my students to do in out-door exercises. Do not send others to do what you are not yourself prepared to do. In your spare time let the Devil find you TOO BUSY for him to meddle with you and then you will not easily find yourself where you ought not to be, nor get into scrapes and mischief. This type of occupation will save you from many temptations.

9. *Straightened Means.* An ever present difficulty to the Native Teacher is the financial bogey. Too often a teacher (and this applies particularly to married teachers) is so worried over the responsibility of providing for himself, his wife and children, that he cannot do justice to his work and then follow the bad report, the warning, and perhaps the loss of his situation. Even if the teacher is drawing enough to live on, there is in many cases the fear of an unprovided for old age. I wonder sometimes if our European friends who are

78

accustomed to dealing with uncivilized Natives realise how hard it is for us to "make both ends meet." We have adopted European habits, our wants have increased, we believe that the satisfying of those wants is a step in our evolution towards a better and fuller life, and yet they give many of us wages less than those given to many uncivilised Natives in the larger towns. You are all familiar with the situation, but it is not easy to suggest a remedy. It seems to me that we must first of all deserve these increased salaries by our increased efficiency and our superior worth, and then must bring our just claims to the notice of the authorities. To achieve the former it is necessary for each individual to live up to the highest ideals of his profession, and in order to be able to present our case we should all join in a Teachers' Association such as this, and then ask the authorities to receive a deputation. We must organise, organise, organise, and be prepared for a long struggle before we convince the Government of our rights in this matter. We shall of course always be modest and polite in our attitude, and never use any but constitutional means.

The Native Teacher and the Church. You teachers therefore should seek not only to overcome these obstacles, but to realise the importance of your position in your Native community, to recognise your duties to your benighted people and to make a real mission of your calling, because the teacher is one who constitutes a connecting link between the manifold secular interests of the village and the Church. It is through the agency of our teachers that the ideals of civilisation and Christianity are going to be transmitted to our masses at large. For our Native schools are, and will for a long time yet, be under the control of missions; and I think that missionary auspices of the right kind are

79

very helpful. Now as we are products of Mission schools we are ipso facto children of the Church. But one meets teachers who will have nothing to do with the Church. They think, and think wrongly, that the Church is not practical, and that its aims are intangible, dreamy and emotional, because devotional. Let me endeavour here to disabuse you of any misconception or wrong notions that you may perchance entertain on this. The Church has always aimed, and I think has been largely successful in this, at making decent men and women of all of us. So that at this transition stage at which South African natives to-day find themselves, instead of being ill-behaved, disrespectful and haughty in consequence of the small education they have had, they are admittedly courteous and humble citizens. It has done much to purify and elevate our talk, where otherwise we might have been addicted to obscenity and slander. It has strengthened men philosophically, where they might have allowed themselves to drift with the stream of fate and fatalism into dismal pessimism whenever they suffered failure. It has done a great deal with its Templary organisations to subdue the twin sins of drink and immorality, where many to-day would have ended their lives as drunkards and dissolute wrecks on the social rubbish-heap. It has taught us to know God and how to live in communion with Him.

These are not airy and empty dreams but solid, uplifting, helpful and severely practical achievements. And therefore it behoves you, if you are to exercise your true power in your villages, to make yourselves allies of your various churches, whatever denominations you may belong to. Seek to be lieutenants to your Priests or Ministers.

Parents. Next to the Church seek to develop the most practical and fruitful relations with the parents of your children and with those of the best rank in your centre. You will thus render yourselves important members of your community. Get to know the homes whence your scholars are drawn, learn the sort of discipline they have grown up under, so that you may thus be enabled, out of the social relations you have established, mutually to consult with them on problems that generally arise concerning their children and secure their co-operation, goodwill and support in your doings. Enlist their intelligent interest in all the matters affecting your school; in this way you will command their confidence in all your undertakings to improve the school. Identify yourself with all movements in the village that are for the amelioration of society. Be present whenever the parents congregate for useful ends, and be ready and obliging to lend your guidance. If you are a man do not shun the Headman's kraal, however backward he may be, but work to win him over to your side wherever possible, giving him the respect due to his office and dignity. Do not be a stranger to the meetings of the men in your village. If you are a woman, make it a point to keep in touch with the unions organised by the women, and their social and other gatherings, for the sake of knowing the mothers of your pupils socially.

Finally, I would enjoin the ideal teachers in our Native communities to be in every sense public-spirited; they must cause their fellowmen to feel that they do not merely "teach to live" but "live to teach," for it is in these ways that they can best and most fruitfully serve their people, their country and their God.

SELF CULTURE FOR THE NATIVE TEACHER.

An address delivered to the "King Teachers' Association" at Emdizeni, Debe Nek, C.P., November, 1919.

I now propose to address Native teachers on another phase of their life, namely, the ways and means of attaining progress, with the object of stimulating you to move forward with the march of civilization. And therefore I desire you to note the following ten points so that you may bear them in mind throughout your course as a teacher.

1. I shall begin with the word *Progress*. By this is meant the act of moving forward as opposed to that of standing still or marking time. The great and harmful tendency of the profession of teaching is that from its similar daily tasks it is liable to degenerate into a monotonous routine and the teacher is too apt to forget the important fact that he is an agent and pioneer of civilization in his location. Take the houses in which teachers are satisfied to live. Are they any different from those of the common-people in outward appearance or inside arrangement? In my travels up country I have observed ¦that the teacher's house is almost as conspicuous as that of the minister for external effect and interior neatness. Who can distinguish in our villages here where a teacher dwells? In fact I know of one teacher who lives in a mud-house which he built forty years ago, and which is now in a state of considerable dilapidation; yet he is apparently satisfied with it!

2. *Departure from tradition.* Now unless you resolve to depart from primitive conditions progress is impossible. To-day you must not rest satisfied with what satisfied your fathers in their days. Move with the times and seek to improve your houses as well as your persons and belongings. Do not stick to a thing just because it was

82

the custom of your parents. On the other hand I do not intend that you should throw overboard everything that belongs to the age of our forefathers; for some of their customs were the result of long experience. The early missionaries razed everything of our people to the ground and the consequence is that in our transition stage we now often sigh for some of the valuable and moral tenets of our tribal and communistic life that served to secure discipline in those days. Therefore in your departure from the old do not fling away everything; but rather examine closely into all things afresh and convince yourselves of the soundness of the reasons why you elect to retain or reject this or that custom. Use wisdom in your selection and see to it that the things you keep are better developed than they were when you succeeded to them.

3. *The Teacher's Position in Native life.* To form a correct estimate of such things you will have to understand and realise what the true place of a teacher ought to be in Native Society. In our stage of civilization the most important person in our villages is by general agreement the minister of the gospel. But when I compare the present with the past, say twenty five years ago, I call to mind quite a number of teachers whose influence among the people was not less than that of the minister. I conjure up names of men now on pension whose record of constancy in their work is not inferior to that of many Native civil servants of repute also on pension

These men did not change schools quarterly as the present generation do; but they stuck to their posts until they saw two generations of the scholars they had trained. Their name became an "institution" in their several districts. A side of life which present day teachers need to be constantly reminded of is their dignity and reputation. One could almost wish that teachers had a distinctive dress corresponding to the ministerial collar. It would serve to remind them of their position for they need to realize that they have in their hands the responsible task of shaping the careers of the men of to-morrow. A vivid sense of this accountability would probably save many from carelessness and lethargy. A serious teacher can even to-day make himself as important as the minister for he, by daily contact with his pupil, a contact lasting in many cases over a number of years, can impress his personality on them in a way a minister·can hardly hope to do on his flock. I therefore wish you all to raise your heads and look to the skies and develop lofty ideals and a serious purpose.

4. *Stumbling Blocks.* And in order to understand what lofty ideals are, you must first rid yourself of narrowness, smallness of mind and limited vision; and overcome a number of obstacles which I call stumbling-blocks that necessarily stand in the way and bar the path of many of you to progress. First let us take *sectarianism*, the church divisions which have made many Christians almost regard one another as enemies. Many black people do not believe in one who does not belong to their church and they think that those outside their denomination cannot get to heaven! To-day many native locations of 400 inhabitants have five sects or more whose members spend most of their religious activity, not in spreading the Gospel to the heathen, but in trying to induce those of other churches to leave their church and join theirs, or in despising the other sects—a woeful waste of energy. The time has now come for us to do away with this mutual hatred on religious grounds and rally round the banner of Jesus Christ for its own sake, if we mean to make progress. Next, let us consider the stumbling-block of *jealousy.* Oh! how

many blessings have you black people lost through your being blind to facts when you are blinded by jealousy. When you see a native rise a little above the rest do you not at once try to pull him down by detraction? Look at the white man, he joyfully praises another white man who makes good. Remember that our model of civilization is the white man, and you must in the same manner admire and encourage other black men who are doing well. Let us not despise the ideas that come from a young teacher just because he is young. Let us not disbelieve a teacher because he is not a favourite, nor from our own district; but let us widen our horizons and behold the wonders of knowledge. Then there is racialism. Alas, how many great and noble causes have collapsed amongst us just because of our attaching excessive importance to the antiquated division of races into Xosa and Fingo, Tembu and Baca, Zulu and Suto, Swazi and Chwana, etc.! These tribal distinctions were perhaps useful in primitive times when the fact of belonging to a particular tribe meant favour at court, cattle, land, and happiness. But to-day we are all under the white man and he legislates not for Bacas and Fingoes only but comprehensively for "Natives" as from the Native Affairs Department. The evil of it lies not in difference of name but in the assumption that the difference connotes enmitv. The time is now ripe for us to treat one another as fellowmen in unity. Watch our Prime Minister who in all his speeches deprecates racialism and yearns for unity. If unity is good for Europeans, it will be even better for us and more necessary. Let us then unite in obliterating the mutual animosity arising from race distinction that some people delight in. Lastly, I take another notorious hinderance to progress: *our desire to be all leaders.* Many of you have seen the apt illustration that recently appeared in our native paper of a team of oxen borrowed from different kraals which failed to pull the wagon, because they all happened to be the leading oxen with their respective owners. We cannot all be leaders and office-bearers in our associations. Some of us must, with our superior ability, be content to remain in the background obscure for the sake of the general cause. That is what the white men do, that is why they succeed, and that is why we cannot go wrong if we follow their example. The secret of their unity and strength is :—

5. *Organization.* The word organization is so common-place that it has become devoid of meaning to many of you. I will endeavovr to give you illustrations. In the Cape Province there are $1\frac{1}{2}$ million white people, of whom probably three-fourths live in towns, leaving not many who derive their livelihood from farming ; yet the farmers alone have about fifty agricultural associations all united by a Congress, meeting annually. We, who are four times as numerous, have practically no such organization nor one so perfect in machinery. True enough a new Native Farmers' Association was stated in 1918 with such success that it has produced no small revival in agriculture amongst us and we still hope for great things therefrom. If you read the official year book of South Africa (price 3/-) you will find that white men have 15 trade unions, some with 1,000 members ; these belong to Plasterers, Engineers, Carpenters, Black-smiths, Ironmoulders, Bricklayers, Plumbers, Engine-Drivers, Miners, Typographers, Coopers, Boilermakers, Painters, Masons, and Printers. They are so powerful that the tailors in Johannesburg are united in demand-ing £45 a month—wages that exceed the yearly salaries of many native teachers !!! How is this done ? By organisation. Another instance : the European teachers have lately come in for a substantial rise in salary under the Administrator's Ordinance. Do you think

this was done as a favour. No. It was by dint of a long organised agitation, of which one used to read many years ago. In the end some of them even threatened to make an organised strike. Their voice was so insistent that it was at least heard by Government. But the Native teachers have never been organised. Government is not easily moved by sectional appeals, especially appeals from people whose voting numbers make no difference in electional results. Another example: The Grey Hospital, in King Williams Town, founded for the benefit of natives by Sir George Grey, has now been turned into a school for whites whose organisation has petitioned Government to legalise that atrocious injustice, whilst we natives being unorganised have failed to petition Government to prevent it. Worse than that we are not ready to organise; nor are we willing to do so. Therefore we are fast losing all the blessings that we could otherwise easily hold and secure for ourselves by this means. Of course, I should mention that there are small attempts being made in various districts, but I must leave this point by saying that, although the unjust condition of the salaries of native teachers—in view of the enchanced cost of living and in view of the general rise of wages in all trades and professions—is a standing disgrace, it remains nevertheless a sad reflection upon the commonsense of the native teachers themselves that on account of their unwillingness to organise they are still unable to remedy this grievance. They are now left to bear their burden until they grow to realise that, after all, their salvation lies in their own hands. You can begin at once in your own district to organise a teachers' meeting for every five mile radius, and multiply your branches.

6. *Growth in Knowledge.* Out of every 100 native teachers that one meets, not more than five show signs of having added anything to their stock of knowledge

87

since passing the T. 3. examination. Their speech, writing and school work betray stagnant minds. Doubtless it was this fact that led Sir Thomas Muir to conclude that the native brain is not capable of following the higher studies of matriculation and post-matriculation work. He said the native mind after the age of 18 suffers mental exhaustion, "mental saturation" as he termed it. I need not take up your time in explaining how recent successes of natives in these selfsame higher studies have, since that statement was made, completely disproved Dr. Muir's theory. To-day neither in newspapers nor on the platform are we lectured, as we used to be, on the inherent mental incapacity of the native. Wrong as Dr. Muir was in his estimate of native mentality he was worse mistaken in the policy that he evolved for the development of native education. He was mistaken in at least three ways: (1) in his introduction of the colour bar both in the classroom and in examination; (2) in lowering the standard for natives in the pupil teacher syllabus; and (3) in confining the native to one and only one avenue of education, namely the teaching profession, completely ignoring the agricultural, industrial and other possible lines of training. This opens up a controversy which one can discuss on its merits, but I merely mention it to show that I for one do not blame the average native teacher for his failure to grow in knowledge after leaving the training institution. The fault lies with the system of education that has produced him and ultimately with Sir Thomas Muir who fabricated that system. It is a system that leaves its teachers with no taste for reading nor for further self-development. It is too low, being equal to virtually nothing higher than a Standard VI. education plus three years of insubstantial theory of teaching. Nothing could be more effectively calculated to ruin educationally the native, because those who possess such a qualification will naturally tend to think they know something while they know nothing. Therefore you as progressive people should constantly work to make up for what you have lost through this faulty system over which you have no control, by using all the means at your disposal to improve yourselves. See to it that you spend your evenings in private study or private reading : Have a time table for this. Keep a list of books to be read. Take care that your information is supplemented by your own private notes and that it is regular, systematic, conscious and accumulative. Get one or two of the newest books on education, say from those recommended for the syllabus of the T. 3. Senior and T. 2. and make it your ambition to learn at least one new theory on teaching, every day, as, for instance, the new theory on the size of classes. The reading of newspapers is valuable also. A progressive teacher acquires from his reading at least one new idea every day and one new idiom in the English language. With such a method of reading you will be surprised what five years' systematic work will do for you. I know of two teachers who in this way can actually speak and write better English than a certain matriculated native. A person who does not aim at development of knowledge soon, like a waterless tree, grows stunted and mentally atrophied. European graduates, in general, acquire more and more knowledge as they grow older ; for University studies compel the graduates, by the habit once acquired, to seek endlessly after knowledge ; hence inventions and what is called research work. Professor G. E. Cory, of Rhodes University College, Grahamstown, is supposed by many people to be a Professor of History, just because he has lectured so often and written so much on his hobby subject of History, whereas in the Rhodes University Calendar he figures as Professor of Chemistry and Metallurgy.

7. *Travelling* is an education in itself if the traveller is a person sensible, sensitive, observant, deductive, teachable and ready to learn from the new and unfamiliar. Within the last six years since I returned from England, I have visited all the large towns of the Union—Cape Town, Kimberley, Pretoria, Durban, Ladysmith, Bloemfontein, East London, Port Elizabeth, Grahamstown, Queenstown, etc., and have seen more of this country than many of you. So that I am probably qualified to speak to you on this subject. There is a story in circulation about a teacher born and bred in Kaffraria, who took his training at an institution there and has since been teaching for a number of years, but has never yet seen King Williams Town. I cannot say whether the story is true or not,—perhaps it is not,—I can hardly believe it,—nevertheless it will serve my purpose for it is probably an exaggeration of the fact that many teachers here and elsewhere in the Union allow year by year to pass without seeing any district but their own; without seeing how other Bantu races live; without knowing the progress made in other locations; without knowing of the superior houses and possessions of rich natives such as may be seen in the Orange Free State native reserves, and other marks of progress among natives in these districts. Such teachers are bound to be limited in their mental horizon, parochial in spirit, narrow of vision, dwarfed in commonsense, puerile in ideas, and often careless in attitude. Now once a year Government allows teachers the railway concession privilege of travelling half price for a return journey, however far they may choose to go. Many use this for going a distance of only 40 miles! Possibly that is due to limited means, as your department pays many female native teachers less for one quarter's work than a white bricklayer earns in a week.

Howbeit those of you who wish it may now save up and spend a week every year or so in Bloemfontein or elsewhere, getting completely away from your locality and for a small sum of money witness instructive sights such as will destroy the conceit that one's own house or location is equal to the best native habitation. The expense is not waste but profitable investment; for you will widen your circle of friends, refresh your health, learn how the other half of the world lives, obtain a right perspective of things and learn to "know thyself." The success and elevation of Japan to a first class world power is due largely to the travelling of Japanese students in Europe for educational purposes. Peter the Great who raised Russia out of barbarism, learnt the arts of civilisation by travelling in the more enlightened countries of Europe.

8. *Attendance at Conferences.* When I visited the United States of America in 1913 I was struck by the great number of conferences, congresses, civic clubs, commencement exercises, secret associations, summer and winter schools for teachers, religious conventions, business leagues, music societies, and many other species of assemblies including banking, political, insurance, templary, missionary and concerns which were attended by thousands of civilised black men who travelled 800 miles and more every year to attend them. All members were humble and anxious to learn from the other members. On account of this attitude the progress of American negroes in all paths of civilisation is faster than that of any other race, black or white, that I know of in the world.

You will at once see, without much amplification of this on my part how important it is for you native teachers to get yourselves into the habit of attending big meetings; for in them you are sure to collect much knowledge, sure to get your intellect stimulated, and become inspired by new confidence as a result of contact with thoughtful and earnest men. Often your services may be valuable and you may thus be able to contribute to the success of your nation, for you can never progress by sitting on your lone antheap (according to the Premier's phrase) while men are deliberating on vital issues in conference.

9. *Activity.* On asking certain teachers how they spend their evenings I have discovered in many cases that they have nothing to do in particular and so, feeling the monotony of unoccupied time weighing heavily on them, they ago about the community visiting friends of various degree of intimacy and relationship, some suitable, some otherwise, and thus drift into wrong company and develop drinking and other evil habits. How best to utilise one's leisure hours is a difficult problem for the teacher more than for any other class. The solution of it by everyone is fraught with far-reaching results, and it depends on activity of the right kind. For you may be indeed active but possibly mistaken. If you read in the South African Native College Calendar what students are expected to do outside school hours you will be amazed at their endless activity, for every hour of the day, in fact every minute is allocated to some useful occupation. Similarly, all teachers of the progressive sort should have a time-table for their activity. In another sense they should take an active part in organising and helping to develop organisations by throwing into them their full energy. Remember that half-hearted activity does not achieve much. It is willing and keenly enthusiastic action that counts in this world. Half-hearted people always find fault with others and are eloquent in enumerating reasons and excuses why they do not

achieve anything. But the energetic man, even if at times he makes mistakes, does in the end achieve something. It has been said, and truly said, that a man who never makes mistakes never makes anything at all. Therefore in any organisation you may belong to, do not play the part of a sleeping member but that of an active one. For instance in your church, whatever denomination it may be, resolve to be an active person. In any association of which you are a member, be an industrious, strong, reliable, indispensable, indefatigable member, always ready with ideas and suggestions. Activity is a formidable enemy to the Devil for the Devil gets on with idle and unemployed people best. Activity is thus a moral weapon. Study your personality discover which way your talent lies, develop and use it to the advantage of your people.

10. *Motive and Ambition in Life.* Those of you who have been on a steamer know that the sea is a huge expanse of water without any road or railway or visible mountains to guide the ships that travel on it. The sun, the stars and the magnetic needle often constitute the only link between life and death for seafarers. A certain geographical point has to be kept in view or in mind and then followed. So with the life of the teacher. There must be some reason, some driving power, some object aimed at as the goal of his teaching and of his life on earth. When a cow dies we say that is the end of it : for we do not know of any ambition it may ever have had in life beyond eating its food. But books may be written of a man and his great exploits and his effort to attain his ambition. It is essential that you teachers, as leaders of a generation, guiding it out from the realms of ignorance and superstition into the kingdom of wisdom and science, should be men and women with specific objects in life for the purpose of developing your own selves and others. Therefore,

93

teacher, set yourself some serious aim, some noble ideal in life, then pursue it relentlessly in and out of season. Endeavour, if possible, as Professor James says in his talks to teachers, never to lose a battle. In any association of which you may be a member do not indulge in unnecessary and pointless speaking in the discussions but think seriously over the significance of your membership and endeavour to make every utterance of real value.

Emerson once said "Hitch your wagon to a star," and it is very wise counsel, for if you aim at the stars then you are not likely to finish up too low in your efforts. Let your standard be a very high and excellent one and you will thus fortify yourself against falling into the ditch. In conclusion, remember that our country, our people, to-day stand in need of teachers and other people with thinking qualities, of men and women who will cultivate sanity and humility. May all our Native teachers in this district and in other places be ever found on lines of serious personal endeavour for the sake of their own people, and thus be truly progressive in every sense of the word.

NATIVE EDUCATIONAL NEEDS.*

With Special Reference to Manual and Agricultural Work, and the Religious Side.

This subject is at once immeasurably wide and of deep interest to all thinking citizens of the Union of South Africa ; therefore, in the necessarily circumscribed space that is available here, one can hardly do more than make a bare explanatory catalogue of some of the points that

---

* A paper contributed to the "South African Ambassador," Johannesburg, February, 1920.

urgently await solution. The problems may be conveniently grouped under (a) Academic training, (b) Industrial training, (c) Manual and Agricultural training, (d) Discipline and Control, and (e) Religion.

(a) *Academic training.* 1. Thousands of native boys are employed by their parents in the blind-alley and degrading occupation of herding cattle. This difficulty can be solved by the fencing in of all commonages and fields of native villages or locations. Government can and should assist them to do this. 2. The time has now come for some measure of compulsory education for natives, because the theory of "keep the native down" is gradually but certainly being given up, as it is being realised that a submerged proletariat tends to demoralise the white man himself. Many white farmers openly confess that it is their reliance upon untrained native labour that has put the agriculture of this country at the bottom of the scale in all civilisation. 3. The syllabus of native elementary schools needs overhauling, and for this we are impatiently awaiting the publication of the Native Education Commission recommendations. 4. The inspectorship in some parts of the Eastern Province is out of date with its policy of terrorism over teacher and pupils. In one case in a school of 71 only four pupils were passed! By all modern canons of education, this cannot possibly be a right and correct index of the capacity of scholars. Something must have been abnormally at fault with the inspector for his system to render such a result possible. A leaf ought to be taken from the first number of the *Native Teachers' Journal*, published by the Natal Education Department (under Dr. C. T. Loram) where a humane inspectorship seems to obtain, typified by sympathy and progress, as shown in its summer and winter schools for teachers. 5. The present qualifications of native teachers are equal to a Standard

Six education, plus three years' training in school method. The lowness and absurdity of such a certificate needs no comment. 6. In one native institution the application of a native to teach in the Normal classes with the requisite qualifications was rejected on the grounds of colour. This leaves a bad impression on natives, as it means that the positions to which they should legitimately aspire are being closed against them in their own schools, being reserved for a white trades union. 7. There is a need for secondary schools to feed the new Native College at Fort Hare, for at present only Lovedale High School does this. The College itself needs support in the way of scholarships and endowment if its development is not to be retarded.

(b) *Industrial training*. It seems the policy of our native industrial institutions that the native is to be trained not to be independent and to compete on equal terms with white artisans, but to fall somewhere short of that stage. Tuskegee and Hampton have much to teach our schools in this line, for they turn out dressmakers and business men of all manual vocations, whilst the training in school includes practical scientific cooking and housekeeping for all girls, elementary agriculture for all boys, and kitchen gardening, poultry raising, etc., for all alike.

This I have elaborated in a report made for the Union Government in 1913 on "Tuskegee Institute" when in America.

(c) *Manual and Agricultural training*. 2. In our schools "manual labour" consists of sweeping yards, repairing roads, cracking stones and so on, and is done by boys only as so much task work enforced by a time-keeper, and under threats of punishment. It is defended because "it makes for character training." The invariable result is that the boys grow to hate all manual work as humiliating, "skulk" from it whenever they can, and ever avoid it at home and in after life. In Tuskegee all pupils are given money for all labour of value—it may be 1d. or 2d. an hour—this being given not in cash, but credited in their bank books. This is excellent in its results, and no labour is despised in Tuskegee nor elsewhere by its students. At the Native College the system of individual vegetable plots of twelve by six yards, in which students share profits with the College is popular.

3. Agriculture, where at all attempted in our schools, has suffered, too, for being made a motiveless task. It is the most important thing in native life, and therefore deserves a place in the school career of our boys, as it is practised in the Mariannhill native school in Natal. How to make agriculture efficient is the most practically important problem for us. Native ministers and teachers could substantially supplement their stipends and salaries if taught gardening and intensive agriculture. This is proved in the Qanda American Baptist School, Middledrift, C. P. We need a native Booker Washington to galvanise natives to action in this matter.

(d) *Discipline.* My ten years' experience with English schoolboys has shown me that to keep native boys in order is a mere bagatelle compared to keeping the former; but they need just as much sympathy if strikes and disorders are to be averted. More use should be made of the native staff members in keeping discipline, especially in view of the growing anti-white feeling evident in boys' talk. There can be no effective teaching without effective discipline. These simple-looking boys and girls are quite sensitive on questions of injustice, and therefore it is men with professional qualifications as educationists and disciplinarians, apart from being clergy and graduates, who should be in control of them.

97

(e) *Religious training.* This training can be administered in mission day schools best by a Christian teacher working harmoniously with a zealous missionary. In the institutions the numbers are so large that this training is not easy, and consequently there has developed much formality, notwithstanding the yearly examinations in religious knowledge. In my opinion boys and girls need to be constantly impressed by means of private religious classes and distinctly religious education by their principals and staff, with the fundamentals of the Bible and the practical life of religion. The staff must establish an atmosphere of an earnest religious tone, for this has lost ground as compared with a generation ago. It is not sufficient to rely upon the morning and evening prayers, the Sunday address, the Sunday class or school, and the weekly class. If these establishments are to justify their claim to being "missionary institutions," then the staff must be somehow selected from sincere Christians with distinct evidence of the missionary spirit, who will preach silently by the example of their life and brotherly love to their pupils in practical fashion. This can be best done by getting teachers from the missionary training centres in Europe, for it is sad to admit, South Africa produces very few people with the missionary spirit, even among the children of missionaries themselves.

Once the type of teacher is correct, then religious training can be left to take care of itself.

Part 3.

NATIVES AND AGRICULTURE.

Address to the Rand Native Welfare Association, University College, Johannesburg, 17th December, 1919.

In dealing with the question of Natives and Agriculture I lay claim to no special training qualifying me to speak with authority; nor am I unmindful of the many burning questions, economic and political, that grieve and rankle in the soul of the African; but for the two reasons that (a) it underlies practically all the problems connected with Native life in this land, and (b) it is the one subject which a mixed assembly such as that facing me, representatives of all sections of the community, black and white, can consider and discuss without losing temper or true perspective.

According to the new science of Civics, Agriculture ranks as the third out of the four stages of the upward development of civilisation amongst the nations of the world; the primitive stages being the hunting and pastoral, whilst the final is the industrial. It was at the agricultural stage that the Bantu were found by Europeans during the sixteenth and seventeenth centuries, while the Bushmen were in the hunting stage, the Hottentots in the pastoral. Now the attainment of the Agricultural stage by the Bantu is an achievement of some merit rarely recognised nowadays by certain reckless and uninformed people who glibly refer to these people as "barbarians and savages" equal to wild animals. One of the romances of this country that must delight the heart of an anthropologist is the fact that all the stages of primitive life and those of modern civilisation have adequate representation side by side. Out of this has sprung a problem: how to adjust the

99

white man's modern industrialism to the black man's primitive ruralism. That is the problem we are to consider now. It is a problem of infinite mystery if studied academically; but, if we confine ourselves to a few practical phases of it, we may reach a position in which we may be able to offer practical schemes towards a solution.

(a) Let us take mine-labour first, and ask these questions: What brings the mine labourer here? Why are their terms of service so brief and intermittent? The answer, I believe, is that the mine labourer comes here just because his wants are unsatisfied at home. He must have money to meet his taxes, to purchase cattle for his Lobola and, most of all, to pay his debts, or those of his people, with the local country trader. For thousands of Natives, as a friend told me not long ago, move in the vicious circle: starvation at home followed by debts incurred with the trader for grain, then a period at Johannesburg for obtaining ready cash, the return home to pay the debts and to live for a brief month or two upon the marginal balance, which becomes exhausted and is again succeeded by want of food and debts with the local stores, and so on, again and again. Manifestly they go to work purely for the purpose of meeting definite needs, not because they believe that continuous work is life's duty. And they all have a germinal ambition to rise and become later in life, something other and higher than merely unskilled labourers. Contrast this with the British labourer who knows that he is destined to live and die a workingman, so that in the coalmines of Wales and the potteries of Staffordshire there is no difficulty of labour supply, nor of "join" bureaux.

(b) In towns there is a large class of Native people, born and bred within the municipality, completely cut off from tribal life and environment, and living by

100

semi-skilled and skilled occupations as well as by service
and clerkships with professional Europeans. Their
housing conditions are often not of the best and for the
work they do they have never received any training,
hence cooks and messengers boys are largely drawn
from the reservoir of an unintelligent proletariat.

(c) Worse is the story of the land, the methods of
farming that are pursued in Native reserves and the
supply of black labour for white farmers. The position
is eloquently, if humourously, described by three
experts on Native Agriculture and Native Social Questions: Rev. Bernard Huss B.A., author of " Agriculture
for South African Natives;" Maurice Evans, author of
"Black and White in South East Africa," and C. T.
Loram, M.A., PH.D., author of the "Education of the
South African Native," all by some remarkable coincid-
ence, belonging to Natal. This is what they say:—"A
walk through the fields of Natives often presents a sad
sight. Amongst a forest of flourishing weeds some
poor cultivated plants seem to struggle for life, whereas
on those fields the cultivated plants should flourish and
the weeds should fight in vain for existence" (Huss).
Father Huss makes the next three quotations also:
" Agriculture is mainly the work of women. They do
but scratch the land with hoes. When the ground is
thus prepared they scatter the seed, throwing it over
the soil quite at random. (Dudley Kidd in "Essential
Kafir.") "The Native is surely the worst cultivator of
the soil in the world—if there is a worse I do not know
him.......The Abantu are probably the worst agriculturists
and most wasteful occupiers in the world. Their fields
are of all shapes and sizes, the straight line being
conspicuous by its absence, and irregularity is the
rule. Examined more closely, they are seen to be just
scratched with a plough, unmanured, weeded in slovenly
fashion, and yielding scanty and irregular crops.......

Most wasteful and extravagant are Native methods of farming, both pastoral and agricultural " (Maurice Evans). " It would be difficult to imagine a more haphazard and wasteful method of cultivation than that practised by the Natives. Small irregular pieces of land are turned over by the hoe, or in a few cases thinly ploughed up. This same plot is cultivated in succeeding years, and as no system of fertilising is practised, it soon becomes worn out and will grow nothing but weeds. Then another piece of virgin land is selected, and the same process is repeated. The adherence to these wasteful ancestral methods of cultivation in the face of European examples is astonishingly strong." (Dr. T. C. Loram).

The general result of these conditions is that the labour supply for the mines is irregular and unreliable, constantly needing artificial and expensive machinery for its recruitment. For the attitude of the Native towards all work is fundamentally a wrong one. The available supply for the miscellaneous kinds of jobs, semi-skilled and skilled, for which the Native is required is inefficient, because of its lack of training. In agriculture the general incapacity that is shown by the Native is due to the fact that agriculture is not taught in his mission and other schools, while the habit of work has never been inculcated under favourable conditions. For instance, when I was a boy in the training institutions of Morija and Lovedale, we used to be drilled each afternoon, armed with spades and picks, to work for two hours at road-making, road-sweeping, stone-cracking at stone-quarries or at any other such job which appeared to us as aimless, profitless drudgery; for the stones we cracked built no houses nor were we paid for the value of the manual labour. There was no motive in the thing. The consequence was that instead of loving manual work, we grew to hate it for we saw no obviously useful purpose in performing it, and no hope

of reward, and it made us bad workmen, and to adore
living with our wits and the. pen. Contrast this with
Tuskegee, where boys receive pay for all manual labour
and where manual work is glorified *per se*, the outcome
being that every Tuskegee boy seeks for remunerative
manual employment during his long vacation, instead
of idling away the holidays as so many of our boys here
do.

Agricultural labour is growing so scarce that one
who has followed the correspondence of the last three
or four years in the "Farmer's Weekly" paper cannot
but conclude that agriculture in South Africa will
always continue to be the most old-fashioned and lowest
of all agriculture in Christendom unless either, (a) some
systematic training of the Native is undertaken by
government, or (b) the white man abandons "Kafir-
farming," and acts as his own labourer, adopting labour-
saving machinery, taking off his coat as he has to do in
Australia and England, and dispensing with black
labour. I do not think that the white man in this
country, according to my knowledge of him, is prepared
to go as far as this.

The inevitable conclusion is that the black man can
hardly be expected to do all that is expected of him
without being trained in the right way, and even in the
case of unskilled labour, his efficiency must in the last
analysis depend upon his attitude towards all work.
Therefore if we solve the question of proper training,
and that attitude we shall have gone a long way to help
employers of labour whether in mines, in municipalities
or in agriculture, as well as to render the Native a tre-
mendous asset in the country's production.

The main principle that I desire to impress is this:
that the employing public of this country—in towns, in
mines, in farms—should be brought to understand that
the training of the Native in the habit of work is a

paying business proposition. Once they understand this it will not be long before they urge Government to get it done ; for it is the capitalists and the big farmers that have influence over government, and at the same time it is they who need the labour of the Native and who would benefit by his increased productivity. As to the ways and means of compassing this end we may all legitimately differ ; but face the problem squarely we must, if the white races of this land are not to be kept in the gutter, as Washington would say, by themselves keeping the Bantu there.

Let us begin with the Natives at their rural homes, their agriculture, and the degree of their industriousness. What do we find ? We find that they have no system. They live on the absolute minimum that mother earth can yield, and they invariably follow the path of least resistance. They are satisfied to live from hand to mouth. If the crops are sufficient to carry them to the following season, then they reckon all is well. They need to be taught that it would be for their own good to learn the necessity of work, not the " dignity of labour " for that is a hackneyed phrase empty of content and never acted upon by any sane and sober person ; for, when I doff my coat and dig my garden to cultivate vegetables, I do not do that out of the love of the abstract idea of the dignity of labour but because gardening pays me economically and physically : there is money in it; it is a necessity ; it is a sound business proposition. This is the attitude we need to instil into the black man of South Africa ; and from what I have seen in the case of Negroes elsewhere I think it is possible and practicable.

In the greatest agricultural producing country, the United States of America, I discovered that progress there was due to the fact that the entire population, black and white, was inured to the habit of work. Nobody there shirked work as many people here, both black and white, seek to do.

At Tuskegee, Alabama, I found that Booker T. Washington owed his phenomenal success as an educator and social reformer to the practical methods he applied in his school whereby he taught the American Negro the commercial value of manual work—methods which are being copied, though to a very imperfect degree, everywhere in the educational world. For instance he divided his students into two groups: one group attended the normal classes on Mondays, Wednesdays and Fridays; while the other went to work at one or other of the forty available vocational industries; then on Tuesdays, Thursdays and Saturdays the first group went to the industries where the theories learnt in class where, by correlation among the staff, carried out in practice, and the second group went into academic classes. While they were engaged at the industries and ordinary manual work, they were paid at so much per hour—however nominal the sum—for all work of commercial value, the various instructors assessing the money according to recognised standards. Two things resulted from this original and wonderful system: firstly, this system produced men and women of economic value to the State, secondly, students became hardened and inured to hard work and loved it on account of the gain and profit to be got from it. Both these results are conspicuous by their absence in the South African system of education. Booker Washington has proved that a sound system of agricultural training in secondary schools can pay for all the boarding expenses of a school. This has been done on a small scale by Rev. J. East, at Qanda, Middledrift.

Whilst waiting for public opinion to mature and for

Government to take action, some Natives in the Eastern Cape Province have organised a Native Farmers' Association and Government has been good enough to grant them an American Negro farm demonstrator of considerable abilities in this kind of work, the Rev. J. East of Middledrift, C.P. This demonstrator who had mastered the dry farming system at his home has within an incredibly short time been highly successful, being a source of inspiration to many Native husbandmen. The Association in its work and discussions has revealed many facts that go to prove the urgent need for Government to assist Natives in their agricultural endeavours if they are to be rendered a productive asset to the Union. Here are a few :—

i. Commonages in all country villages are overstocked and hundreds of cattle die each year because the inhabitants have by a natural increase of population outgrown their old areas, while the labourers from the Rand keep adding stock that the pasture lands available cannot possibly carry ;

ii. The land ploughed by location individuals is far too small to provide a living. It averages from four to six acres per family in the Ncwazi location of four hundred inhabitants, a location whose entire size is less than the single farm of a European neighbour. It would be interesting to know what sort of a living the average white farmer could make out of five acres with his family and all. Yet that is what the black man is trying to do.

iii. The implements used in Native farming are old-fashioned, inadequate and often unfit ;

iv. The ox-traction that they depend upon is a handicap, because very few possess the requisite number of oxen to enable them to prepare their lands. Single-ox and single-horse traction is wanted ;

v. Fencing is required, if modern agriculture is to be

attempted, otherwise with the location cattle roaming loose in winter it is impossible to develop winter crops;

vi. There are no dams nor other means of water supply in locations;

vii. Sanitary arrangements are nil and the present condition of promiscuous veldt defecation favours disease and plague;

viii. Poverty is appallingly on the increase, and with the present high prices for foodstuffs it is a crying shame on Government that nothing has been done to arrest profiteering, or speculation in mealies, or the fixing of the price as has been done in the case of rice and sugar. Starvation itself is facing many of our people at the Cape and no one has raised a voice of protest in any organised manner against this atrocious condition of things;

ix. The stock owned by Natives, their cattle, sheep and horses are of the lowest pedigree and there is need for foreign bulls and stallions to raise its standard and money value;

x. Astounding ignorance prevails with regard to the simplest rudiments of agricultural knowledge (e.g. soil preparation, crop rotation, manure uses, poultry raising, bacon curing, disposal of produce, fruit cultivation, dry farming methods, irrigation, weeds, insects, tree planting and timber growing, etc.). All this shows a need for training in agriculture parallel to that given to whites in the Government colleges of Elsenburg, Grootfontein, Cedara, Potchefstroom, Glen, with a Land Bank, scholarships, etc., for which government to-day expends yearly about £100,000 in the case of whites and only £500 for blacks whose taxation revenue is by no means proportionally negligible.

In conclusion one would venture to offer the following suggestions as likely to assist materially in the solution of the problem of Native Agriculture :—

(a) A systematic attempt should be made to rouse the enormous inert mass of red-blanketed Natives, who are outside the reach of the educational machinery, into action. This can be done by the extension of the system of black agricultural demonstrators trained at the Tsolo School of Agriculture, or at the Native College, Fort Hare, or better still, trained in the United States through government scholarships. All these three sources could be usefully employed.

(b) Elementary Education from the very beginning should include the rudiments of agricultural knowledge. The Natal Native Education Department has already shown the way and has been highly successful in this line.

(c) In Native Secondary Schools and Normal Training Institutions agricultural training could be immediately introduced to take the place of Woodwork and Carpentry, as being the more useful for the purposes of Natives. This was the evidence given by the Native Farmers' Association before the Government Native Education Commission at the Cape last July. Example here could be taken from the Tuskegee system.

(d) In Higher Examinations the Science of Agriculture should have a Professorial Chair appropriately at the Native College where Native experts and graduates could be produced to train other Native teachers. In this connection see the South African Native Affairs Commission report of 1903—1905 of which Sir Godfrey Ladgen was chairman and Mr. Taberer, Secretary (page 82, paragraph 382) which *inter alia* recommends, firstly that a higher standard of education should be instituted among Natives to increase their efficiency and wants, and secondly, the encouragement of industrial and manual training in schools.

All authorities and employers of Native labour can

and should take a share in having this problem solved
even if for their own selfish ends. Municipalities could
set aside portions of revenue derived from the Native
locations and put up their own establishments, or vote
money towards the present institutions that are struggling
under difficulties to carry this into effect. Mine-owners
could do likewise and use their influence on the Rand
municipality and on government to get something done.
European Agricultural associations could do a great
deal, especially as it is they who suffer greatest from
the inefficiency of Native Farm Labour. They must rid
themselves of prejudice against the black. A small
attempt was recently made in the case of the East
London Farmers and Fruit Growers Association, when
a member of that body submitted a well-meaning paper
to the Annual Cape Agricultural Congress at Queenstown,
in which he made practical proposals for the purpose
of training Natives to become more efficient labourers
for white farmers. Harmless as the scheme seemed it
was unanimously rejected by that Congress, while the
very chairman of the proposer's own Association was
among these who voted against the scheme.

The Government through its Department of Agriculture is in a position to do a great deal to develop Native
Agriculture for which it does nothing to-day except for
a single item in the Native College farm. Public money
spent upon machinery to convert the huge population
of black people in the Union into a productive and
work-loving people would be money wisely invested.

NATIVE FARMERS' UNIONS.

The occupation of tilling the soil is a very old one with us. We knew about it long before white men invaded this dear land of ours. To this day we know much about stock diseases, and for many of the older diseases of cattle we remain independent of Europeans. With the copious and regular rainfalls of the times of our grandfathers it was a simple and sure thing to cultivate very lightly, plant and reap with certainty. So fertile was this dear land. Whenever one part was played out we had abundant land to select from and we went thus from place to place. Gradually this freedom became limited and to-day our holdings, specially in locations, are so small that the old methods cannot supply our needs. We must learn the white man's methods. We should therefore study how to make agriculture a paying proposition and a profitable business, and we must study the ways and means of getting hold of advanced information :

(a) It is a good and inspiring thing to learn from experts, especially from successful black farmers. For instance, I had the privilege of living in close contact with Prof. Geo. Carver, a negro blacker than ourselves, who carried on experiments in the research department of Tuskegee Institute. He had made several discoveries, among which was a method of increasing the yield of sweet potatoes until he had managed to obtain over 500 bushels from a single acre, a phenomenon that attracted the attention of scores of white farmers in the centre of negrophobist Alabama. To live with such men is an education.

(b) There are cheap books that would repay investment, as for example the " Farmers' Annual " that costs only 4/-, but is a gold mine in the way of information.

(c) There are many inexpensive agricultural journals

110

like the "Farmer's Advocate," "Poultry," "Gardening," "The Farmer's Weekly." You could make clubs and combine to subscribe to one or more of these and they would be a home university to you. Or special arrangements could be made with our Native press to have certain columns reserved for agricultural news.

(d) Associations of Native Farmers with periodical conferences where questions affecting the life of farmers could be taken up, would be a boon. For example you might debate the policy of education and how your sons should be given agricultural training in present educational centres; and how you should get Native farm demonstrators to go round amongst you such as those do who are trained in the Tsolo School of Agriculture, Transkei. Printed matter goes a long way and we should read much literature that deals with the problems of cultivation. A recent article in the "Farmers' Annual" dealt with topics such as these: France spending millions of money upon re-afforestation; The "Farmers' Weekly" as a valuable medium of instruction; Waste of Land by Natives; The Future of Natives—their rapid increase above the amount of land available (e.g. Basutoland now maintains half a million Basuto; but in time to come their land will not be able to feed and hold their number.)

Therefore the acquisition of land is of paramount importance just now for without it you will soon be economic slaves. England, according to recent reports, is realising this, for the Department of Agriculture in that country is arranging for three millions of acres to be put under cultivation for the first time. White people in this country realise this, hence they pass laws like the Lands Act 1913 to make hay while the sun shines.

Organisation is needed as a start. White men have agricultural associations everywhere and they receive a Government grant. There is no progressive European farmer but belongs to some association or other. In the Cape Province alone a Congress of these meets yearly and it comprises about fifty branches! In the "Dispatch" one constantly sees reports of the proceedings of some of these and it is wonderful to note the comprehensive variety of the subjects handled in their meetings. Take for instance the agenda of the "Lower Cathcart Farmers' Association" that met at Thomas River on 31st December last :

1. Kubusi Bridge; 2. Dangerous Roads; 3. Scab; 4. Kaffir Beer; 5. Wool; 6. East Coast Fever; 7. Native Affairs; 8. Natives Trespass at Railway Cottages; 9. Erosion; 10. New Divisional Council Ordinance; 11. Bi-Annual Conference; 12. Voters' Roll; 13. Typhus; 14. Attendance of members at meetings, etc., etc.

In fact quite a number of laws affecting Natives may be traced to these European agricultural associations, and it is time we established our own associations even in self-defence if for nothing nobler. Therefore I conclude by proposing that we found a Native Farmers' Association, with Rev. J. E. East as President, for he is a great expert in dry farming and can teach us a great deal in the right methods of cultivation.

The above was an address given to the Natives of Zanyokwe, Rabula, near Middledrift, C.P., April, 1918, on the need for the formation of a Native Agricultural Association.

The meeting eventually agreed to found a "Native Farmers' Association," and its objects are the following :—(1) To stimulate its members to a greater interest in farming; (2) To urge its members to become more productive farmers; (3) To exercise a mutual helpfulness in methods of farming; (4) To secure for its members the highest prices for their produce; (5) To obtain for its members the cheapest prices in buying seeds, etc.; (6) To encourage its members to grow a

112

variety of crops; (7) To be united in approaching the Government on matters affecting the interests of Native farmers; (8) To urge its members to form companies for buying such machinery as forage presses, thrashing machines, etc; (9) To publish or circulate agricultural literature in order to enlighten its members and to further its objects.

And the following address given eighteen months later (7th Oct. 1919) by one of its members is a testimony of the value of this organisation to African peasants. This is how it was published in "Imvo" :—

HOW I SUCCEEDED AS A FARMER.

The following is the gist of a lecture given by Mr. Stephen F. Sonjica, of Qanda, Middledrift, Treasurer to the Native Farmers' Association (Eastern Province) and a man of substance, before a recent gathering of the said Association at Ncwazi, at the special request of the meeting. The story was thrilling in its recital for it was embellished with piquant humour by the narrator. It should serve to stir up many other Native farmers to action.

The speaker said that he grew up under typical mid-Victorian conditions of Xosa life, when a Native boy's life was notoriously no bed of roses, and under an extremely austere father. His parents loved stock-raising to a fault and on the contrary had a laisser-faire attitude towards soil-tillage. His father severely reprimanded him as a boy whenever he ploughed deeply and told him not to "kill" his cattle. Despite these adverse circumstances he clearly foresaw the benefits of the proper cultivation of the soil and expressed to his father a desire to buy land. "Buy land!" exclaimed his father in horror, "How can you want to buy land? Don't you know that all land is God's and he gave it to

113

the chiefs only ? " With this short shrift, continued the speaker, I planned to buy myself land of my own to plough elsewhere. When I announced to my wife my intention of leaving my father's home to work on my own account to secure land, she stood aghast at this, and endeavoured to restrain me from such an unnatural and disloyal idea. This proved futile for I was adamant and determined to go to seek work. Thus I left home for King Williamstown and served as a mounted police-man during the War of 1877 alongside three com-rades. Whilst ostensibly sending home my monthly earnings to my father in the usual Native custom, I cunningly opened a private bank account into which I diverted a portion of my wages without the knowledge of my father. This went on until I had saved £80. At this juncture I visited home and besought my father to lend me cattle to enable me to till some land I had hired. The request was rejected with scorn : " You plough that hired land of yours with your *own* cattle, not mine ! " Just what he inwardly wanted, for he straightway went back to town and bought a span of oxen with yokes, gear, plough, strops and the rest of agricultural para-phernalia, returning triumphantly to his father who was flabbergasted with amazement and asked where he had gotten all these things from. " These are the cattle you told me to get myself," was the brief and unanswerable reply. His father knowingly bit his lips for he realised that his son must have been keeping back much money all the time. For fear of treachery he did not leave his cattle with his father but deposited them with a friend near town. Now he resigned his position in town although his three comrades tried to dissuade him from this, and staked his life on farming. The start was try-ing and hard beyond description—to save the expense of hiring labour he put his wife to the plough and drove the oxen himself, turning a deaf ear to the insistent

114

murmurs and loud protests of neighbours. The harvest was not encouraging either, for it totalled only seven bags! His three comrades laughed at him "We told you so." The second year yielded only nine bags and his opponents were now justifiably confirmed that "Fani" was truly mistaken in his venture. Not he. *Nil desperandum*. The third year brought him thirty-nine bags. Now he told his wife to stop ploughing and return to the house and he hired helpers. The fourth year placed ninety bags into his barns. His three comrades and other critics were now silenced once and for all. The fifth year produced one hundred and twenty-five bags, and all his friends began to refer to his wife as "Mrs. Sonjica," and automatically ceased to call him "Fani," but styled him "Mr. Stephen Sonjica." *Labor omnia vincit.* He had made good. He bought a wagon against the advice of his father and within a short time he had accumulated £1,000 in the bank by means of farming. (Loud Cheers). "I now purchased a small farm," continued Mr. Sonjica, "and plots of land at various places at what was considered high prices in those days. Agriculture has continued to raise me higher and higher since those days, and I cannot too strongly recommend it as a profession to my fellowmen and encourage those in it. They should, however, adopt modern methods of profit making. For example the way Natives at present dispose of their produce in local shops is a glaring scandal. No native farmer is worth calling a farmer who has no agent in a big town through whom he may dispose of his produce at market prices. "A farmer without an agent in town is not a farmer but a boy!" I reckoned to know all about the art of ploughing and preparation of the soil. Indeed I do it as well as Mr. East himself. But there is one point where Mr. East beats me : that is in scuffling. His system of one horse scuffling is the most profitable proposition that I have learnt of late years. It took me a long time to appreciate its value and to learn how to manage a horse with plough and reins alone in Mr. East's style. At first Mr. East visited my farm and scuffled several acres with his one horse within a short time, and I became convinced of the value of the new system, and brought one specimen made at his black-smith's shop. It played ducks and drakes with me in the using for the horse would not keep straight and I abandoned it in sheer disgust for twelve months. Next year Mr. East tried again to teach me and I succeeded. His method saved me the enormous expense I had used to incur in hiring scufflers. It gave me joy for it showed me to what good use one should put horses in one's fields. Unto all of you therefore I say, go and do likewise, casting aside indolence, developing industry and stability.

NATIVE PEASANTS AND THEIR DIFFICULTIES.

An address by the Native Farmers' Association to M. C. Vos, Esq., B.A., the Secretary for Native Affairs, July, 1919.

By a special arrangement for which Rev. J. Henderson, M.A., Principal of Lovedale, was responsible, the Secretary for Native Affairs, Mr. M. C. Vos, B.A., held a meeting at Burnshill with the Native Farmers' Association on Saturday, July 12th, 1919, when there assembled a representative gathering of Native farmers drawn from all the districts extending as far as Peelton and Healdtown in one line, and from Keiskama Hoek to Perksdale in another. On the platform there were: Mr. M. C. Vos, B.A., Rev. J. Henderson, M.A., Mr. A. B. Payn, M.P.C. of

Tsolo, Lieut.-Col. E. H. W. Muller, Treasurer of the Transkei Council, Mr. G. Whitaker, M.L.A., of King William's Town, Prof. Alexander Kerr, M.A., Principal of the Native College, and Rev. W. Stuart, M.A., of Burnshill.

Mr. Stuart in choice words welcomed the distinguished visitors, and Mr. J. E. East, the Government Farm Demonstrator, briefly outlined the objects of the Association, emphasising that the great aim was to solve the food problem as expeditiously as possible.

Then the Association's address to Mr. Vos was read in the Xosa vernacular and interpreted in English.

It ran thus :—

We, the Native Farmers' Association (of the Eastern Province) express our sincere gratitude to you, Sir, for having granted an audience with you thus early after your appointment to an important department which we Natives regard as a trustee of our welfare. To-day thousands of eyes are fixed upon you, and thousands of black hands are outstretched suppliant to your bureau for succour and relief in these perilous times. Sir, you have visited us at a time when the Natives represented by this association are in a grave plight. We are suffering severely from an unusually protracted dry season. Many of our homes are absolutely destitute of provisions, on account of the failure of the recent crops, and our prospects of a wheat harvest grow dimmer and dimmer as the drought continues. Our cattle are dying daily for want of pasture. And the cost of living has risen excessively, whilst the wages Native farmers command at the mining centres and elsewhere have not risen proportionately—in fact at the mines they stand at pre-war figures. Again the dreadful typhus fever is exacting an alarming toll of our people, whole districts being almost entirely without medical attendance. Notwithstanding these gloomy circumstances you have come

117

to us at a time when we are feeling jubilant over the victorious peace that has ·been concluded in France; a peace which we hope and trust is destined to spell progress and justice to all mankind.

As a society of Native Farmers we desire to place before you, Sir, some of the great difficulties that confront us in our struggle to ascend in the scale of civilisation.

1. The first cause of difficulty that we would point out is the inadequate size of ploughing ground that is at our disposal individually. The average of our allotments is six acres each ("isikonkwane"), and the rainfall allows of only one crop. Therefore if we grow wheat there remains no place for maize, the staple crop. The maximum crop of mealies these small plots are capable of giving in the best of seasons is thirty bags (value fifteen pounds), an amount which cannot possibly feed nor clothe a man's family, pay his taxes, school fees, and so forth. One has only to visit a typical location like Rabula (near Keiskama Hoek), where they have an average of from thirty to forty acres each, to realise the advance that Natives can achieve in civilisation, when given adequate ground. Under this head we would recommend an inquiry as to the amount of land necessary for a Native to support himself under present-day conditions.

2. Our next difficulty is that of limited commonages. This very day immense numbers of our stock are dying from this evil.

3. The need is being felt for the establishment of a system that will secure us the following desiderata: (a) The construction of water dams in the various locations for the service of people and stock ; to-day both man and beast have to travel unconscionable distances to reach water in many a community. (b) Methods .for

118

getting a better breed of stock, with farms for same. (c) Fencing material for enclosing our commonages; the lack of this is a very serious set back to Native agriculture as, during the winter months, cattle roam at random, and no aspiring farmer dare attempt a "catch" crop such as peas. Moreover commonage fencing would release thousands of boys for school and other purposes, whose time is now wholly and deplorably consumed in herding stock. (d) The development of local afforestation so as to obviate the primitive method to which our women folk are compelled to resort in order to gain firewood; such forests would incidentally provide building material, as they do in the Transkei, and pave the way for improved Native housing. (e) The training of a number of Natives for the medical profession, (say, on the lines suggested by Dr. J. B. McCord and Dr. C. T. Loram in the African Journal of Science, January, 1919 number) to deal and cope with the multifarious diseases that are responsible for an appalling death rate among Native landdwellers.

From your department we have learnt that some system is in operation among the Transvaal Natives whereby advantages similar to the above are obtained through voluntary taxation without the formation of a Native Council such as that of the Transkei.

4. Another obstacle is the lack of a good market for Native produce. The local trader generally acts as an emporium where the Native sells his crop, and where he is compelled to take value in kind and receive no cash. As these shops have a monopoly, and as the law protects them against competition from additional shops, we feel, Sir, that the law ought also equitably to insist upon their giving cash and that according to market prices less carriage. We would request Government to fix the price of the sale of mealies on the same lines as that of sugar and paraffin.

5. The present system of dipping gives the Native farmer no little heart-burning on account of its glaring injustice. In the first instance we were told that the Government was making a loan for building our dipping tanks, to be refunded in instalments by means of a five-shilling additional tax on each taxpayer. Now, after the completion of the refund, expensive European supervisors were placed over the dips and the five-shilling tax continued. Moreover by this system the man with no cattle has to pay as heavily as the one with many cattle; the man with two cows the same as the man with fifty.

This we hold to be unfair and unjust. The tax is proving to be an excessive burden on the backs of a starving people, and is more and more becoming a source of unrest. Also there is no uniformity in its application, hence its partiality. We understand that the South African Native College is prepared to train Natives in testing and supervising dips, and therefore to lighten the burden we suggest that such Native supervisors, if trained, be appointed to this work, and that an explanation be made periodically as to the amount of money raised and how spent in dipping.

6. Mine Labour.—In view of the fact that Native farmers who sign on here for labour at the mines possess no means for having their wages increased at the other end on account of the nature of their contracts, we should respectfully suggest that the question of an increase in wages be given speedy attention, as at present they remain at pre-war rates, while that of the European in the same work has been advanced greatly in keeping with the cost of living. The granting of this request would greatly help Native farmers at this time.

7. We would suggest the encouragement of village industries to alleviate the distress due to congestion of Natives on the land.

120

8. Agricultural Exhibition.—We would suggest that the Government encourage and aid the holding of an Agricultural Exhibition at Lovedale in order to stimulate greater interest in Native agriculture.

9. It is highly desirable that suitable agricultural literature in the Xosa vernacular be made available for Native farmers in the same way as it is for European farmers in Dutch and English by the Department of Agriculture.

We feel, Sir, it would be a grave omission if we failed to inform you of the destructive in-roads poverty has made in our locations during recent years. The number of our cattle has steadily decreased till many of our kraals are empty. Only a few years back each man had his own span for ploughing and some to spare. To-day, in most cases, it takes the cattle of several families to make up a team. This is a great draw-back to Native agriculture. This shortage in our cattle is due to our selling them for food, as we are not able to grow enough on our small plots during the repeated droughts, and also, to inadequate grazing lands. Many, indeed many, are insolvent, and this evil is increasing yearly. As the traders see our stock diminishing, they are fast becoming reluctant to give us credit. There is also a large number of indigent widows in our locations facing starvation, who need immediate help.

In conclusion, Sir, having informed you of our grave condition and many hinderances, we pray that they may receive your beneficent consideration, and that your coming to us to-day may result in a redress of the many evils that we have to combat as Native farmers.

Done by order of the Native Farmers' Association.

NATIVE VIEW OF FARM LABOUR.

A defence addressed to various newspaper editors in South Africa by the Native Farmers' Association, February 1920.

Sir—With your kind permission we desire, through the medium of your valuable organ, to make a defence in behalf of the Native so much belaboured of late by press correspondents and others.

Wilfully misleading statements constantly occur in the press under headlines such as "Spoilt Kaffir," "Starving Natives," "Native labour," and so forth, from the pens of Europeans, calculated greatly to shake the confidence of aborigines in the ruling races of this country. We are informed in and out of season that the white man is the guardian and trustee of the black man, and that the interest of the black man is safest in the hands of the white man. But if we are to judge the whole white race by the opinions expressed in the daily papers from time to time, then we must conclude that our future and destiny must be awfully doomed.

(1) Much is being said against education and Christianising of the Native people—that the schools and Church are spoiling them—these expressions emanating not only from individuals but also from reports of associations. The opinion seems to be gaining ground, specially among white farmers, that the raw Native is of far more service than the one from the school and mission. The truth is that the spoilt party is not the black man, but the class of white people who have been getting, and wish to continue getting, the labour of the Native for a mere song. Who has forgotten how the Native labour battalions in France performed within twelve hours what was reckoned a fortnight's normal work for European labourers? For generations the raw Native has done service for his

122

white master for a bare pittance—some for one beast a year (according to some venerated old Dutch custom) and his ignorance was such that he hardly knew when his year began or ended. In the Colony a common custom among European farmers is to give 10/- a month (i. e. £6 a year) with a dish of mealies a week plus some sour milk, the wife and children of such a servant giving their service *gratis* to the employer. The class of people who render such service are raw or " red," in the blanket stage, having no school fees nor church dues to pay, no clothes to buy for their children who move indecently clad about their master's estate, and, not infrequently, the adults being insufficiently apparelled to be presentable at any civilised home. Sometimes a mealie-sack with a hole cut out at the bottom for the neck and with the corners cut open for the arms constitute the sole garment of a male adult servant (!) inasmuch as his wages could permit nothing better. Now these servants rest contented while they plough their master's land, milk his cows and tend his stock. The master through this cheap labour soon becomes opulent and flourishes about in a motor-car.

The position is quite different with the school Native. He wants clothes for his whole family, money to pay school-fees, better food, sugar, coffee, tea, bread sometimes and some modicum of furniture. His needs cannot be compassed by £6 per annum and therefore he cannot compete in labour with his raw brother who has few needs. Further he wishes to be in a locality where his children can attend school. It is the school and Church that have made him like this, and therefore he is termed the " spoilt Kaffir "—not because he is a thief, robber, or a murderer, but simply because the conditions offered by his master will not enable him to lead a civilised and Christian existence.

That Europeans ever did get this cheap labour is to
123

be deplored for they have been spoiled by it, as was evidenced last year by the wail that came from an ex-South African settled in Australia who from the antipodes sighed for this cheap 'Kaffir labour'! Our white friends need to adjust themselves to the new status of the Native rather than to seek to drag the Native back to the primitive life they have outgrown once and forever.

(2) Some of the articles on starving Natives have been largely erroneous and misrepresentative of the facts. Certain writers would have us believe that Government is feeding, free of charge, robust and able-bodied men who are too lazy to go and offer themselves for work. This is not the case. Only indigent widows were supplied with poor rations in these parts, and that only after the most careful and searching investigation. It is true that numbers of able-bodied men are also to be seen about Native locations, but it is the "Join" Labour system that is largely responsible for this phenomenon, for these men are signed on for contracts, of from nine to twelve months at a time, to the Rand, and are then brought back home in huge numbers, at the end of their agreement, to spend two or three months at home, and then join up again. It would be patently absurd for them to come down all the way from Johannesburg, working their own fare as they do, to spend just one day at home and go back again! This is the logical conclusion of the hare-brained statements that find their way to the press. The obliquity of the Rand Join system can be realised when one compares it with the period of time Natives labour in Cape Town and Kimberley, whither they proceed without contract and spend anything from one to five years on end. Very often it is the labour agent and others interested in such occupation who are most brazen-lunged in urging that these people be compelled to join up, for they receive about £2 on each

" boy " registered for the mines, while they sit at home grow fat and do nothing ; for some of these agents earn £100 a month through these poor Natives who can hardly save £10 a year; and yet they have anything but a good word to say about the creatures that bring them such wealth. The farmers too are crying out against the Government supplying grain to Natives, because they wish economic pressure to force the Natives to go to their farms as cheap labour where conditions degrade them. In some cases Government is not giving away grain but supplies it to be paid for by a certain time. We regard this as a very gracious act on the part of Government, seeing that Native crops have failed ; but our callous critics call this "giving food free" because it suits them, as they want Natives to be forced as cheap labour to their farms.

(3) Native labour. There is a persistent cry over the lack of Native labour, specially by the farmers, as they feel that they are not getting their proper share of the labour supply. The root of the trouble seems to be in the price paid for labour. The Native to-day has developed intelligence enough to know which side of his bread is buttered and to know where his labour commands the best pay. In the mines and towns two to five shillings per day are given for unskilled labour, but the farmers offer a very much lower figure. It is for them to raise their price of labour and treat their servants humanly and humanely and then they will obtain abundant labour. The farming community doubtless must assume a different attitude towards Natives if they wish to secure a reasonable share of the available labour. In the Cape Provincial Farmers' Congress of last November, representing some fifty agricultural associations, a novel proposal, original whatever its limitations be, was made to the effect that a scheme be launched to train Natives with Government

125

help in ploughing, clean cultivation, reaping, trenching, hoeing, milking, etc., with the express purpose that farmers might be able to get more proficient servants. This proposal, be it noted, was not to the end that Natives should be trained to help themselves in their own land, but to the selfish end of supplying white farmers with more efficient labourers; no books were to be taught as in ordinary agricultural institutions, no experimentations or analysis of the soil as in Elsenburg, but just the dry bones of the thing, simply how to use the hands more skilfully in tilling the white master's ground! The scheme, this tiny crumb of training, was holus-bolus rejected by an almost unanimous vote. The cause of the opposition is revealed in an animadversion by the president of East London Farmers' Association who is reported thus in the " Daily Dispatch " :—

"The President referred to Mr. Goulden's motion re Native labour which was submitted at the recent Agricultural Congress at Queenstown, and apologised to Mr. Goulden for having voted against the proposal. He was forced to do so, because he was strongly averse to the education of Natives. He maintained they should be kept in their proper place, and should not be placed on an equal footing with white men. He considered there was a tendency to degeneration among the Natives, and his opinion was that they would die out like the Hottentots."

According to this hackneyed order of thinking the proper place of Natives is evidently to remain in illiteracy and heathenism. On the other hand if the training outlined above could really put Natives on an equal footing with white men then this president has betrayed himself by showing that his ideal of a white man's agricultural education is a very simple one indeed. The attitude of his Association, as press reports disclose,

126

is that of enslaving the Natives. Their desire to have their servants legally contracted and to have Natives carry passes; their objections to Natives buying land, owning land, hiring land, squatting on European farms, being educated and evangelised, being advanced food on credit or even having their indigents fed by Government lest that hinder Natives from being unconditionally forced on their farms as servants—all this connotes absolute slavery and serfdom for the Native people of South Africa. And after noting the attitude of the Queenstown European Farmers' Congress we wonder how far this negrophobism and mania for seeking to reduce the Native to servitude has affected the rest of the white farming community of the Cape. We are, etc.,

Native Farmers' Association, Eastern Cape Province.

WHY NATIVE FARM LABOUR IS SCARCE.

(REASONS AND SOLUTIONS.)

As a consequence of the daily press reports of the Johannesburg address on Native Agriculture the present writer was summoned to East London to meet a committee of the East London Farmers and Fruit Growers' Association at the National Hotel, 13th February, 1920, for the purpose of the mutual exchange of views and frank discussion upon the causes of the scarcity of labour, as well as its poor quality when at all available. There were present Messrs. Freer, Goulden, Adkins and the Hon. Secretary, Mr. W. R. Goulden, whose report in the "Daily Dispatch" in part runs thus: "The chairman introduced the Professor, expressing the pleasure they felt that the natives had amongst themselves a gentleman who so willingly gave both time and money to further the interests of his people. They heartily welcomed him and his co-operation in the ultimate achievement of securing a reliable and efficient class of native on the farms, in which trust and confidence could be placed, for they were prepared to pay anything for this class of labourer; but not for the useless type.

" Prof. Jabavu thanked the committee and expressed himself as agreeably surprised to find, having heard their opinion, that they were working in the same direction as himself. Where he had anticipated unreasonableness, as evinced in the reports published of statements made by some of their members, he was glad to see that they were out for a fair and square deal with the native. On the lines indicated he would be very pleased to give all possible assistance. At Fort Hare there had been introduced with very great success the encouraging of a love for gardening amongst the scholars, and it had taken root: now there was a spirit of emulation, one competing with another to see what they could produce. When these students went out to work they would, at all events, know something about the soil and how to use it."

During the discussion it was found that the causes that accounted for the scarcity of Native farm labour were enormous. They may be divided into three sections, under (1) Treatment, (2) Wages, (3) and the attitude of Natives toward farm work generally, whether for themselves or for employers.

(1) From information gathered by enquiry when at Pretoria, Johannesburg, Bloemfontein and in various places in the Eastern Province which may be reckoned as reliable, the consensus of opinion is that there is a noticeable change in the present generation of white

128

farmers as compared with those of former times, the tendency now being towards hardness and lack of consideration towards their workers.

A certain well known Native in Bloemfontein told me that he had not very long ago undertaken to recruit labourers for farmers in the Orange Free State and the Transvaal, and that he was forced to abandon the venture on account of the unfavourable reports brought back by the workers from the centres of employment. These men said:

(a) When ill-treated they found that they were absolutely in the power of the "baas" and had no umpire to appeal to who could guarantee them humane treatment. (b) There was no security for them to be conducted safely home, such as they enjoyed under the Rand recruiting agencies; hence some had been known to disappear completely either by death or by becoming lost in the broad country, when endeavouring to get back home, in consequence of illness or physical incapacitation. (c) The rule of the "baas" is so arbitrary and merciless that he imprisons them even for minor and trivial misunderstandings. (d) They were liable to sudden evictions at the caprice of the Dutch farmer. and under the Native Lands' Act of 1913. (e) There were many cruel and hard taskmasters who indulged in whipping and other form of physical chastisement.

Near the Alice district one middle aged farmhand informed me that in his time Natives really loved farm labour for it was rendered congenial by the kind of masters they used to have. But that to-day (a) there had come into being a new generation of white farmers bent upon enormous money making and proving ruthless; and their unfriendly spirit towards their servants had led to their forfeiting their confidence as a class. (b) Farm labour to a black servant to-day offers no prospects for chances to rise economically and socially,

129

because most of his old sources of profit and savings have now to be diverted to the master's. For example his stock is limited to a very small margin; all his surplus stock must be sold to the "baas" and at the baas's price which in cattle is £7 for a £15 beast; the cream from his stock has to go to the master as payment for the privilege of running his stock on his lands. (c) Living quarters are miserable, especially in the rainy season, as compared with those in town locations (d) The food is only "inkobe" (boiled hard maize) with no meat except for a chance dead cow—this comparing unfavourably with the varied food enjoyed by the town labourer. (e) Dismissal is instant and unconditional as compared with the month's notice in towns.

(2) *Wages*. i. The pay offered by farmers is far lower than that obtainable say at East London or Cape Town, where unskilled labour commands anything between 3/- to 8/- a day, and even 10/- at Port Elizabeth on occasions.

ii. No option is given for cash payment.

iii. It does not cover the expenses of clothing, school fees and church contributions.

(3) The attitude of Native youths towards farm labour.

i. They have grown to regard it as a sort of low, mean and disgraceful occupation, in contrast with being a teacher, a clerk, a minister or interpreter. At Thaba Nchu I found quite a number of young men who owned about two thousand morgen each of land in the Native reserve who, instead of farming, had gone into towns to live as teachers and pass-office clerks, earning only from £50 to £80 a year, where their lands could yield them a minimum of £1000.

ii. They have grown up in their homes under conditions where agriculture is a failure, offering no financial returns to meet their modern needs and ambitions.

iii. They are discouraged by the frequent droughts, as they have no method of fighting them through their ignorance of dry farming principles.

iv. They have no taste for agriculture, for, apart from the crude and fragmentary ideas they pick up at home, they are taught nothing about. it at schools, either elementary or secondary.

v. In seeking occupation they, rather than take up farm labour, prefer Cape Town, where they find three obvious advantages : (a) The attitude of fairplay from employers, the Peninsular Europeans being proverbially good and kind. (b) Proper notice in cases of dismissal, as against summary treatment at Johannesburg. (c) They find Cape Town conditions morally helpful to one who is a trier.

(4) *Suggestions.* To undertake to write out a complete prescription for what would produce farm labour is as hopeless a task as that of defining what electricity is. But we need not despair, as this is a matter of life or death to the earnest farmer. So let us look at some possible ways of tackling the problem :

i. The social relations between the farmer and his servant have much to do with the supply of labour, says our Lecturer in Agriculture at the Native College, Fort Hare, Mr. P. Germond. He holds that the white farmer should discard the "stand-off" attitude that is so common and do more friendly talking with his farm hands, study their individuality and encourage them in the habits of thinking, inventiveness, originality and resourcefulness in solving the innumerable troubles and difficulties that constantly arise in connection with farm stock and implements. His experience is that by adopting a teaching attitude, for example, by asking the labourers the why and wherefore of things, as in fence-making, one can do much to quicken the otherwise dormant intelligence found in every servant. And servants trained in this way usually glory in being useful and become reliable enough to be left to do their work alone.

ii. Wages. Whilst some cash is necessary, the farmer should seek to prove to his servant and succeed in satisfying him that the acreage given him to plough for himself, and the free pasturage plus the cash he gets and free housing, are quite equal to the 3/- per diem obtained in towns without these advantages. Natives with families prize the facilities of education for their children and church going for themselves.

iii. Elementary Education in Native schools should be so framed that it habituates Natives to farm work from the lowest standards. The Natal Native Education Department, under Dr. C. T. Loram its head, is doing this with great success in the form of garden plots attached to Native Day Schools. Farmers could advocate that this method be made universal in all Native schools in the Union, even from their own selfish point of view.

iv. In Secondary Schools for Natives Tuskegee ideas of giving prominence to Agriculture in the training of all boys could be easily applied in this country, if farmers could undertake to educate public opinion on the point. For example in Tuskegee the Negro boys are taught agriculture in all its branches, being trained to develop a taste for varieties of vegetables, to turn their produce into cash, to attend agricultural shows, and to use the most up-to-date traction methods, with the result that the motto for success among the Negroes is " forty acres and a mule " for these produce wealth and an automobile. The system of horses and mules is far quicker, more convenient and time saving than the oxen traction of South Africa, with its long process of the collection of bullocks from the distant veldt, the laborious inspanning and

132

the multiplicity of servants (the driver, the plowman and the leader boy) instead of a single man for all those jobs. In fact Mr. East, the black demonstrator around Middledrift district has trained a number of Xosa boys who are now quite experts in managing, single-handed, a couple of horses, and tilling with them huge tracts of land in far less time than cattle would take, and who are equally adept in manipulating the American single horse-cultivator that is patented and manufactured by Mr. East himself at Qanda, Middledrift. Mr. East has also achieved considerable success at the Native College at Fort Hare, where he twice a week trains the male students in individual garden plots, teaching them how to raise from seed, develop and market a great variety of vegetables, while at the same time inculcating in them a taste for this kind of food and work.

v. On the basis of the preceding information it would be a paying proposition for European farmers to lay aside racial prejudice and pursuade the Department of Agriculture to systematise the teaching of agriculture to Natives.

vi. For the purpose of centralising farm labour European farmers could establish labour agencies parallel to those of Taberer and Mostert in the case of the Rand recruitment, or that of the Natal sugar plantations. In this way their labour would be regularised. Preference should be given to men with families to be taken on long and definite contracts, as these men having a stake in their farm settlement would the most likely to prove reliable as compared with irresponsible youths.

vii. Conferences with leading Native people, where frank round-table discussion was encouraged, would do a great deal of good, not only towards the actual supply of labour but in building up good will and understanding. The most influential class of people among the Bantu just now is that of the ministers, chiefs, headmen and teachers, and once the confidence of these is enlisted and their co-operation is secured in periodical conferences one can see nothing to hinder the achievement of the full solution of the problem of Native farm labour.

TEACHING NATIVES HOW TO FARM.

To the Minister for Native Affairs,
    Government Buildings,
      Pretoria.

                                3rd December, 1919
Honourable Sir,

We, the Executive Committee of the Native Farmers' Association, have been directed by our association to call the attention of your department (as we had already done in our memorial to the Secretary of Native Affairs on the 12th July last at Burnshill, Middledrift, C.P.) to the alarming rapidity with which poverty is growing among, and pressing upon the Natives in our districts, due (1) to the enormous loss of stock and failure of crops, (2) to the fact that they have very small holdings, (3) to their ignorance how to utilise such holdings to the best advantage, and (4) to the limited commonages.

The association feels that there is a crying need for a Native agricultural school that will definitely specialize upon the best methods of cultivating such small holdings as are possessed by Natives, and inculcate in them the futility of overstocking present commonages.

Our feeling is that a great deal of good could be done, if there existed some large experimental or practical school-farm divided into small plots, such as could be successfully worked by one horse on intensive lines,

134

as done by the one-mule-and-thirty-acres system in the Southern States, U. S. A.—each student being provided with one horse and a plot to be used under proper supervision (for we are told by those in a position to know that one mule or horse could plough a much larger extent of land than the average acreage possessed by Natives in these parts). The prevailing ox traction system is proving an absolute failure as through the heavy losses of stock from droughts and shortage of grass, few Natives have cattle sufficient to constitute a span of four oxen wherewith to plough, while on the contrary they have many horses in the locations, which are of no farming value on account of our people's ignorance of horse-agriculture. One horse is said to be of more economic worth than four oxen as a traction power in agriculture.

Native people around here have been astounded by the possibilities of horse agriculture as seen through the performances of the demonstrator from the Southern States that you have so graciously supplied for the members of our association during the last twelve months. Our association also sees a great opportunity for making the Natives a great asset to the country in the line of poultry growing, if this were taught them in a practical farm-school. Pig-raising and bacon-curing on a modest scale would greatly add to the value of such a farm-school, for Native people have not even a rudimentary knowledge of these common industries which would mean a great help in the present crisis. The amount of agricultural training and the number of farm schools open to Natives are, in the opinion of the association, not at all commensurate with their numbers and the taxes they render towards the country's revenue ; and they are in dire need of this kind of training and such schools.

Never in their history, not even in Nongqause (which

135

in effect was a localised and circumscribed disaster) have the Native people generally been faced with such a serious economic crisis as they are to-day. Through the recent drought they have lost a large percentage of their cattle; through their ignorance of dry-farming and using methods unsuitable for their small holding their last year's crops failed. Many homes in our district are without food. The Native hospital in our locality, being over full, is daily turning away scurvy-stricken patients due to underfeeding.

Should you think it wise, Sir, we would be glad to meet a representative from your department for a frank round-table discussion of the above suggestion.

With all humility, we remain,

Your loyal servants,

Native Farmers' Association.

NATIVE VILLAGE INDUSTRIES.

An editorial from the Lovedale *Christian Express*, April, 1920.

The Governor-General's speech at the opening of Parliament frankly admits that a new stage has been reached in the development of the Native races. The progress achieved demands new opportunities. We invite an expression of opinion from missionaries and others in touch with native life and thought, and from educated Natives who read the *Express*, as to whether the time is ripe and opportune to start, in the areas where the native population has become too dense to live by stock raising and agriculture, industries financed conjointly by whites and natives and worked on a profit-sharing basis.

The colour bar and segregation amply justify such a

136

departure. Many natives are quite capable of doing skilled labour; were they allowed to do it, their earnings would be increased. If the white man denies to them the right to do the skilled labour they are capable of doing on the mines, he cannot have the face to say that they shall not do it at their homes. To give the natives in their own parts of the country suitable and remunerative employment would result in a large measure of *voluntary* segregation, which should help to obviate the clash between white and coloured labour and greatly benefit the native by keeping him away from the degrading influences of town life, as well as by making it unnecessary for him to break into his family life by long absences.

The spirit of the age is calling for profit sharing—that the man who by his hard toil wins the wealth should receive a fair share of that wealth. This has been in large measure conceded to the white man. Is it righteous to deny it to the Native? If we sit still and allow this injustice to be perpetuated without making a determined effort to put it right, are we not culpable? Cain's world-old question, "Am I my brother's keeper?" is but a sorry subterfuge.

Our suggestion is that a limited liability company be floated to establish suitable industries for natives in areas where the population and other conditions warrant. That a capital sufficient to see the venture well through its initial stages to successful production be subscribed and called up as required. That interest on shares be limited to $7\frac{1}{2}\%$, any profits beyond that figure being divided into two equal parts, one to be distributed among the native employees who have worked steadily throughout the year, the other being placed to an extensions fund for new developments. Provision should be made in the articles of association to prevent any capitalist buying up a controlling interest in the company when it has reached a paying stage, by limiting the holding and voting power of any individual to, say, one tenth of the subscribed capital; or in any more effectual way that can be devised.

One great advantage in making a start at the present time is the high cost and scarcity of manufactured articles, and the apparently remote prospect of production overtaking demand, or of prices falling. Various industries suggest themselves with which to make a beginning. Perhaps that of spinning and weaving might be tried first. Wool from native owned sheep might be purchased throughout the Eastern Province and Territories and made into blankets for which there is a big market among the native people. Later on tweed might be manufactured and a clothing factory established also to meet the native demand for decent and suitable clothing.

By manufacturing the wool locally a whole series of profits and commissions and freights, as well as import duty, would be saved to the natives, from the time their wool clip leaves them until it comes back in the shape of blankets and clothes; moreover the wages for manufacture would be retained in the country instead of being paid and spent overseas. It is probable too that the article turned out locally would be more free from shoddy or cotton than that usually supplied for the native trade; and we might hope to be delivered from that abomination so much in evidence—the cast off clothes of Europe patched up for native wear.

That spinning and weaving can be carried on successfully in South Africa has no longer to be proved. It is being done already and at a good profit; but on a scale which can only meet a fraction of the demand for European requirements, leaving the greater demand for the requirement of the Native untouched.

What results might be looked for from such a venture?

If our vision comes true, regular and good wages with a share in any profits will have a marked effect on the progress of the native employee. We may look for a rapid growth in self-respect, for better houses and a better home life, better food and clothing, better education, better support of the Church and of missions to other parts of this continent.

No doubt short-sighted farmers and other employers of native labour will be inclined to oppose any development of this kind because of its tendency to raise native wages. But they will come to see that cheap labour is, in the long run, the dearest because it is inefficient: that it is true economy to employ fewer, but more intelligent and capable, men at a higher wage: and that after all it is a pretty low down ideal for a white man to set himself, that of growing rich on the labour of the native, for whose social, intellectual and spiritual advancment he not only makes little or no provision, but whom he selfishly wishes to keep down as a helot.

To whom may we look to launch such a venture as we have outlined? Letters received on the subject from laymen in Britain show that, in their opinion, it is up to the Christian business men of South Africa to shoulder it and carry it through. There are in the Eastern Province, and especially in the Border towns, business men of high character and ability, whose family traditions link them to the Missionary enterprise and the advancement of the Native. Might not they pick up the mantle of their fathers and grandfathers and wearing it adapted to this modern Missionary call, take the responsible lead, inviting the Christian laymen of South Africa to back them?

"Lord, give me courage—strength to do the deed
From which flesh shrinks, nor choose the easier way
Of dalliance and self-sparing—Lord, I need
Thy spirit to sustain me day by day,
And give me courage, both to see and do
The rightful thing, whatever else I rue."

139

REPLY TO THE FOREGOING.

To the Editor, *The Christian Express.*

Sir,—The article on "Bantu Industries" appearing in your issue of April 1, deserves thanks of all the better educated natives, both for its practical business insight and for its generosity towards natives. I for one have reason to believe that the time is now ripe for the starting of industries in the thickly populated rural native locations, specially in the areas of Fort Beaufort, Victoria East, Middledrift, Keiskamahoek, Debe valley, and elsewhere all around King William's Town, the Transkeian Territories and Pondoland. During the last six years I have observed several attempts, in the above named districts, by natives in the line of trading, carpentry, boot-repairing, launching of newspapers, basket weaving, broom-making, the making of earthenware vessels, sale of ironwood sticks, and so forth, ending in most cases in failure, loss of invested money, or at best yielding insignificant profit.

Nevertheless the great lesson of these is that natives are willing to be led into the routes of successful business and industry, if they only obtain intelligent and sympathetic guidance from honest experts, plus financial aid for the necessary start. Many white people utilise the constitution-given colour bar not only to degrade the black people politically and socially but to protect themselves in their own trades and professions against the competition of natives whom they are pleased to term their inferiors; hence the exclusion or suppression of natives in skilled trades and in the better positions in the civil service and in the teaching profession (e.g. tacit colour bar against natives teaching in the Normal classes in Native Institutions in cases where they possess the required qualifications, these classes being reserved for a white trades union).

The fact that this scheme will tend to keep natives away from town life will certainly make it obnoxious to the mining magnates, as their profits from labour supply are built upon the poverty of the natives who are thereby driven to the Rand. Against this I may say, as I said at Johannesburg last Christmas, the insufficiency of the native labour supply, its unreliable character, and the bad workmanship of the available labour, are explained by the prevailing system of native elementary education which is too bookish and provides no systematic and sensible training in the habit of regular manual work where at all it is attempted, and none in domestic science and agriculture, the most important occupations in native economic existence. In this connection, Mr. Editor, I wish to support your appeal to the Department of Education in the question of teaching the methods of proper housing to native school teachers, for the Report of the Housing Committee 1920 reveals ghastly facts on the appalling death rate among natives traceable to bad housing. But I wish you had added cookery and housekeeping for girls and agriculture for boys—these to be substituted for sewing, woodwork and drawing, which in my opinion are of secondary importance, a waste of valuable time and really worthless in after life under our present educational system. I hope this will catch the eye of the Department.

To return to the Industries, one would say that your scheme is excellent and deserves publicity throughout the native press (Bloemfontein, Johannesburg, Basutoland, Natal and King William's Town), whose editors might invite their readers to discuss the question and possibly call meetings with a view to giving practical effect to it, for there are many of them who do not see the *Express*, while you, Mr. Editor, might be good enough to draft tentative articles of association for a liability company on the lines of your suggestion, inviting

141

white and black to join. For spinning and weaving and the making of blankets St. Cuthberts, Tsolo, in the Transkei, would seem a favourable centre, as this industry appears to be a success there. An experiment might in the course of time be made in the Keiskama valley.

Such an undertaking would materially benefit not only the natives but the country as a whole, for it is the poverty of the native that is a drag on its economic progress; were he more skilful in trade, intelligent in organisation, inured to the habit of regular work as the American Negro, and more economically independent, he could render South Africa not only richer and more productive, but would act as a stimulus to the white man himself to move on in developing the yet unfathomed wealth of this land.

I am, etc.,

D. D. T. J.

April 1920.

[Re-published with the kind permission of the Editor of the *Christian Express*].

Part 4.

NATIVE WOMANHOOD.

Address to the Winter School for Native Teachers,
Amanzimtoti, Natal, July, 1920.

When I was asked to give you an address there came
to my mind the interesting debate that took place last
night on the "Lobola" custom when I observed that
all the lady speakers were in favour of the retention of
the custom while all the men seemed to be against it.
My aim now is not to take sides on this question but to
try to show you certain aspects of the subject.

The subject of the womanhood of our people is so
important that one would like to awaken your noblest
instincts in the consideration of it. Reference is made
to it, in a brief way, in "The Native Teacher out of
School." Mr. Sigamony, the earnest and patriotic
Indian teacher of Durban, told us two days ago that
"no nation can rise higher than its womanhood"; this
agrees closely with a sentence, in an article by Mrs.
Hertslet in the "South African Quarterly" current
number, which says "The Bantu can only rise as high
as their womenfolk." Is this a plagiarism or a case of
two great minds thinking alike? Then again in the
latest issue of the "Native Teachers' Journal," Father
Bryant contributes an illuminating article on Bantu
social life and shows himself to be a protagonist of the
Lobola custom. A Bloemfontein paper called "The
Homestead" has been opening its columns of late to
correspondence upon the evils of the system of employing Native girls as nurses for children. Also, an
impartial view of this question is to be found in the
new Housing Report compiled for Government. Thus
you see that Native women are being discussed in all

sorts of circles just now. That signifies that we are living in a time of crisis in the evolution of the black race of Africa. Let us look at the subjects from three standpoints.

(a) The significance of the Lobola custom ;

(b) The life of Native women in towns ;

(c) What our attitude towards our women generally should be.

Lobola.

(a) At the Cape, while there are still many who cling to the Lobola custom, there are many Christianised people who have discarded it. Perhaps we may not settle the question here and now, but we can at any rate agree upon our general attitude, if we once grasp the arguments for and against. Let us take the pros. first and then the cons. Those who favour the Lobola tell us that :—

i. Women do not find it a hardship; and this was testified to by the female debaters of last night ;

ii. It guarantees the careful upbringing of girls by their fathers, as girls cannot marry without the consent and choice of parents; hence this is the only way to ensure their welfare during their youth ;

iii. The system endows the wife with esteem in the eyes of her husband, inasmuch as he secures her only after an outlay of much trouble ;

iv. It affords a wife moral protection, because under heathen conditions there is no signed contract against personal abuse ;

v. It acts as a restraining check against the reckless abandonment of the husband by wife as compared with the divorce system among school Natives ;

vi. It places brides at a premium and this conduces to respect, for then they cannot be picked up anywhere and everywhere, as they otherwise can, merely for the asking ;

144

vii. It compels suitors to work where no other inducement can make them get into the healthy habit of labour.

On the contrary these are some of the arguments against :

i. Under this system women are worked mercilessly, specially if childless ;

ii. Woman becomes a commodity that is purchased by the highest bidder, and since this is a purely business negotiation as between parents, there is no element of esteem ; contempt for woman is the consequence ;

iii. To procure the requisite cattle, a young man is obliged to go to the Johannesburg mines often for two or three recruitments and when he returns to get married he develops a feeling of vindictiveness which leads him to ill-treat his new spouse ;

iv. Woman is looked upon as a mere servant whose duty is to cook and build houses for her lord ;

v. As a return for the cattle she must populate the home with as many children as possible without regard as to whether she can properly train them ; hence if she is barren she is a cursed creature ;

vi. The sentiment of love is never considered by the parents who decide to arrange the marriage ; hence the contract being devoid of any noble idealism is calculated to destroy conjugal bliss ;

vii. Polygamy therefore becomes not only possible, since this is a matter of cattle, but natural, desirable, and even idealised ; with certain tribes when a man died his wives were logically killed and buried with him to serve him in the next world.

That is a brief summary of the position. Observe that on the whole the system fits in with people in primitive social conditions where contracts are not executed by written documents but by the tangible form of barter ; and that, whatever present opinion be, the custom is sure to grow out of use amongst civilised and Christianised people on account of its accompanying cruelty and the economic handicap it places upon couples starting in matrimonial life. The European or educated view is that all the parents concerned should contribute to the wedding of their daughter or son, because married life is notoriously a difficult adventure in civilised life, if one starts it with no capital, nor property, nor furniture.

In our Native life the task of providing the ten head of cattle is so heavy nowadays that there are cases of youths who, having gone to mines for two occasions and raised about seven cattle in all, have been driven into despair and have returned home to elope with their financée; others who manage to complete the number incur such heavy debts over the wedding ceremonies and carnivals that the husband has once again to go to Johannesburg to work to pay off these debts, leaving his new bride alone at home; others do not recover from these initial liabilities for, many years. What a contrast this is to a white friend of mine for whom I acted as best man in his wedding: he had all the furniture, crockery, house, piano, garden and all, given as presents by the parents of his young lady and his own, long before the day of marriage. The argument that the Lobola develops esteem for the wife, in the eyes of her husband, may be discarded, for the usual effect is actually the opposite: "I have laboured hard to get the cattle with which I obtained you; your job now is to kindle the fire, cook, and rear children for me." "You must go and plough with the oxen," said the husband of a barren woman in my district, "for you are a bullock too because you do not bear children," and the miserable wife had to perform some of the roughest manual tasks possible under the threatening rod of her inexorable master.

146

Under this system the tender emotions of conjugal love and family affection are purely accidental and secondary, if not entirely absent. Man is everything, woman nothing. Therefore without wishing to constrain you towards one view or the other I leave the facts to you for consideration; study the problem more minutely and decide for yourselves whether the advantages of Lobola are not outweighed by the disadvantages.

Native Girls in towns.

(b) Some months ago a European lady in the Rand created a sensation in the press by making serious charges against Native nurses and women generally employed in towns, saying that these were responsible for contaminating white children and other white people with certain diseases and influences. We need not go into the details of this unsavoury topic but can take the situation in a general way.

When I ventured to challenge the accuracy of this sweeping defamation of our people which was being reflected in scurrilous attacks in a Bloemfontein paper, the reply showed that the authoress had out of her local experience of Durban and Johannesburg made libellous generalisations incriminating black people everywhere in the Union. Such statements, so far as my acquaintance with the whole of the Union goes, do not hold good for all other towns, certainly not for the Eastern Province and the Native territories. Those who claim to be benefactors to our people would do much good if they humbly limited themselves in speech and writing, especially in calumnious matters, strictly to what they know and avoid damaging generalisations until they have mastered their facts and figures.

Now, there are two questions here that face us :—One is, Why do our Native people allow their girls, in very tender years even, to swarm to towns for work? The other is, Why is it that European employers are so careless about the proper housing and the moral welfare of their nursemaids and kitchen servants? Let us begin with the latter question. The white people, who employ Native girls in towns, assume no parental responsibility for the moral welfare of these girls. Specially is this the case at the Rand which is proverbially the cesspool that swallows up all the worst characters of the Union. It is a notorious fact in Native circles that whenever a young man or woman has fallen into mischief and has disappeared, in nine cases out of ten they have fled by train to Johannesburg; hence it is unsafe to presume that Johannesburg conditions hold good for other towns. It is the London or New York of South Africa, the refuge of criminals. European employers however are satisfied so long as these girls discharge their duties regularly. They do not concern themselves with the way they spend their leisure time and evenings, nor with the rascals who introduce themselves to them at their backyard quarters and develop an acquaintance which often leads to their ruin. This is an enormous danger which has been realised by few Native people. Fortunately of late certain European employers in Johannesburg and Durban under the organisation of Mrs. L. Hertslet are beginning to pay serious attention to this problem and it is to be hoped that some tangible result will follow.

As to the other question: do you as teachers ever study the reasons that have led to the exodus of so many of your women from their homes? Is it a good thing? Is it a healthy sign? Can you not do something by advising their fathers and mothers against sending girls to towns without an undertaking from their employers that the demoralising conditions are altered? It is your duty to know of these dangers that are a menace to our people in this critical stage of their social evolution. Remember that these girls, having left the raw state of naked heathenism desire to be dressed in nice looking blouses, skirts and shoes, while the stings of poverty and hunger at their homes, due to the droughts and failures of crops have rendered it impossible for their parents to supply them with the money necessary for these things. Our country girls have developed a great craze for the flashy clothes that they see worn by town girls. This seems to be the allurement of the towns, quite apart from the evolutionary disintegration of the tribal life as it used to be. Black people now have far less control over their children than they used to possess. This is where your help as teachers is required. Ponder over the following words which I quote from the article by Mrs. L. E. Hertslet in the June number of the "S. A. Quarterly":

"The plight of Native women in Johannesburg is a burning question which affects everyone of us and the Bantu races in that the demoralising influences of the towns are threatening to spoil a large number of their Native women, who in their turn will harmfully influence their country cousins. Would that the Bantu might realise the evil for themselves, and stem the tide that sets townwards! Before they have gone but a short distance in their upward march towards a virile national life, the very foundations of their strength are threatened by the danger to their women."

Possible Ideals for our Womenfolk.

(c) An experience of over ten years in Europe and the United States of America has taught me something of the place of women in civilised society—society that can give points to many white people of this land. It was my privilege when in England to make extensive visits to homes that could really be called beautiful.

149

One such home in Somersetshire, where I used to spend some of my college vacations, was equipped with such perfect appointments externally and internally that I ofttimes exclaimed to myself "If heaven is as nice and comfortable as this home then it must be a fine place indeed!" This was due to womenfolk who by their home training were endowed with a taste for the superfine; women who had entered matrimony on terms of social equality with their husband, not as chattels. The British principle in times of danger "Women and children first" was gallantly observed when fire broke out or when there was threat of a ship-wreck. Compare us when we board trains: "Men first, women last." In society it was "Ladies first," an expression that would be regarded as outrageous in one of the Bantu languages. In those countries the luggage of ladies is borne by men, with us it is the opposite. In society woman is reckoned and treated like a jewel, a pearl, a treasure of priceless value, idolised and idyllised in songs.

She is taught how to make herself deserving of the honour and respect ascribed to her. She must do this by cultivating the qualities of grace and beauty, beauty not of face but of soul and character, sweetness of manner, gentleness of speech, kindness to people, specially to those in suffering and trouble—doing this without pride or conceit but in the proper and natural order of things.

Men follow certain definite codes of manners and etiquette such as taking off their hats when greeting ladies; they remove pipes and refrain from spitting in their presence, offer them front seats in gatherings, give them the correct side in walking on pavements, offer them seats in the house, trams and trains, always protecting them and using refined language in their

150

presence—doing this not pedantically nor effusively but naturally in accordance with the code of chivalry.

Lofty are the heights which woman has reached to-day in cultured countries. She has indeed reached absolute equality of opportunity educationally, religiously, economically and even politically.

For instance in the Negro schools and colleges of America there are many more women than men receiving higher education. In a Summer School for teachers that I attended at Tuskegee, Alabama, U. S .A., where there were 400 teachers, there were 350 female teachers and only 50 men. That is why the American Negroes are making wonderful strides in education and civilisation. There is no field of university studies where women have not displayed mental capacity equal to and often excelling that of men. In my own graduating class in London the best student was a woman, one of our lecturers being a lady Doctor of Literature. Many a happy musical "at-home" have I enjoyed at the residence of a London lady who was a Fellow of the Royal College of Organists. In Church work they have gone beyond the limits prescribed by St. Paul, for the pulpit of a famous Holborn chapel is to-day occupied by a female minister, whilst there exists a sect whose ministry is composed of women preachers and ministers. In professions they have invaded even the legal field, there being female attorneys and barristers including the distinguished Advocate Christabel Pankhurst, LL.B. (Lond.); whilst there are many women doctors qualified from Edinburgh and London Universities.

And finally in politics not only have they secured the franchise in many countries but there is actually a member of the fair sex in the British Imperial Parliament itself, Lady Astor, M.P., who from all reports is giving a good account of herself as an orator and politician.

Those are the exploits of which womenkind are capable. They show that the time has come for us to take up a new attitude and grant some respect towards our women. The privileges enumerated above have been obtained only recently, some of them since the war. They did not come through the flourish of a magic wand. Much work, organisation, agitation, imprisonment, hungerstriking and suffering had to be endured by the pioneer women in order to overcome the ancient sex-prejudice. Therefore as teachers we should work to influence public opinion, in our villages and reserves, for better treatment and nobler regard towards our womanhood. This can be done even from a humble beginning. For instance the Native Farmers' Association in the Eastern Cape Province is tackling three vital problems which if overcome should go a long way to release Native women from the unreasonably heavy work which degrades them physically: these are the three tasks of (i.) scuffling in fields; (ii.) carrying fuel from great distances on the heads, and (iii.) fetching water from remote streams.

To combat these difficulties we enjoin members to sow their mealies in rows and use cultivators drawn by two oxen instead of manual scuffling; we instruct them to make plantations around their homes and locations so that wood may be to hand; and to build dams or reservoirs with Government help or to construct tanks or windmills or furrows to lead water by gravitation where practicable. Once the women are liberated from these enslaving tasks they will be free to practise better cooking, to beautify their homes, to bring up their children under their personal attention, to improve their own health and that of the race in general and to have the opportunity to work out life's ideals.

European women and those of other civilised nations have been long ago relieved by their men from these

152

tasks which unduly hamper domestic progress and that is why they have been able to raise their nations and empires ; for it is woman that governs the pace of progress. Therefore if we mean to rise in this world and to command the respect of other nations we must begin by raising up our women. We can do it by educating them as highly as we educate our boys, laying emphasis on domestic training and hygiene where the boys learn agriculture and house-construction, learning and imitating the methods of the more civilised races. We can inculcate the virtues of chivalry upon young girls and boys in our day schools in connection with our moral lessons, not by word of mouth only but by our actual life and practice.

> " Earth's insufficiency
> Here grows to event ;
> The indescribable
> Here it is done ;
> The woman-soul leadeth us
> Upward and on."

SOCIAL REFORM.

This is an address given at King Williamstown, on Friday, 14th May, 1920, to a Native audience. The Chairman of the meeting in question recommended that " in view of the educative, helpful and hortative character of the address is should receive wide publication."

Mr. Chairman, Ladies and Gentlemen,—My first duty is to thank the Committee of the local organisation of the Abambo Anniversary observers who did me the honour to ask me to address this notable gathering on this notable day. Up to this day I have sedulously avoided associating myself with these sectional and racial carnivals on the ground that our people are not sufficiently educated yet to be capable of performing these celebrations without yielding to the temptation of indulging in undue self-praise, self-complacency, harmful references to other fellow Africans and the positive fomentation of racial animosity already a bane among the European citizens in this same land.

Nevertheless I decided that rather than continue in tacit seclusion and abstinence it might be more manly for me to come and speak candidly to you, and explain what my feelings are on such celebrations, even at the risk of injuring the susceptibilities of some who are keen on these things. I have felt that while much could be done in the Fingo festivals, by prudent speakers exhorting their people to noble life, the occasions could easily produce much mischief when narrow-minded enthusiasts turned them to the disadvantage of the other tribes. This remark of course holds good with reference to the other tribal festivals *mutatis mutandis.* For instance it does not follow that because you celebrate the memory of this day, therefore you should hate those who are not Fingoes, or who were once your masters, some your protectors, some your oppressors, some your friends. But this easily happens with people in our stage of civilisation. Another example: many claim that the 14th of May denotes the date of the freedom of the Embo people from bondage or slavery; and yet the Amahlubi, a section of the Abambo, repudiate this as they were never at any time enslaved by the Amaxhosa!

Therefore I wish to preface my speech to-night by pointing out that the only justification I see for the continuance of such celebrations is that they must be used for edifying the whole African race and not a section. We should on these occasions take stock of our present position, study ourselves, plan for the future, study our old customs, and those customs brought to us by white

154

men, and learn the wisest ways of avoiding social dangers in our stage of transition from our communistic life to that of European civilisation.

For our tribal life is going and has gone for ever. We are *nolens volens* learning and adopting the new and foreign civilisation by the very fact of living in towns. This is excellently described in Dr. C. T. Loram's book: "The Education of the South African Native."

To-night, therefore, I propose to take stock of what appears to me to be the chief dangers that threaten socially to destroy us all as Natives (see Daniel 5 : 5, 25), and my remarks shall not be limited to the Abambo or Fingoes, but shall be directed to the whole Native race in the Union of South Africa.

Once we realise the dangers and rocks that lie in our course, our Scylla and Charybdis, and their true importance, as well as learn how to steer clear of them, then it will be possible for our posterity to build successfully upon the foundations that we ought to lay to-day in our social life. Among the things we should study is our history, because most of the present generation do not know it. It is a fascinating story that should make our hearts throb and inspire us to lofty actions. That is one of the values of history for all of us—both the proud and the humble: for if you boast of belonging to what was once a great, lordly, powerful and brave tribe, then to-day you must aim to excel in the noble arts of civilisation, progress, culture and prosperity. On the contrary, if you meekly belong to what was a down trodden people, then you may take courage and contemplate the pitiful negro slaves of 1850 in the United States who to-day lead all black races in culture—(see their wonderful magazine the "Crisis" of New York)—and behold how extensive your opportunity is to make good! Why not then leave behind us printed records of Native history

155

written by black hands—Native history that will be the pride of our descendants? A good number of books containing Native history are to be found; but they are written by white authors who naturally must take care of their own interests first, and one cannot blame them, for blood is thicker than water. Some modest efforts have been made by Rev. J. K. Bokwe, Mr. S. E. Mqayi and Rev. T. B. Soga—(please let me know should there be others): but we are still in need of some serious research work on these lines by a black man who will get his sources from the old Natives themselves, who are fast passing away. Such are the things to which your celebrations might profitably devote themselves.

Now that the Great War is over, the Native Question has once more become the bone of contention in newspaper controversy and on the public platform, and the football of politics. If you follow newspapers, and I know that most of you do not, you will find, firstly, that Europeans who take the sane view of things have become more outspoken than formerly and, if anything, more confirmed as friends of the Natives. To give a few instances, take the attitude of the press in many Union towns, notably the Johannesburg "Star"; take the Rand Native Welfare Association, which has done much good for Natives; take that epoch-making paper of Bishop Furse lately of Pretoria; take the excellent letter of the Archbishop of Capetown recently issued to members of his Church; take the eye-opening speech of the Mayor of Stellenbosch, Mr. P. D. Cluver, and the illuminating paper by Dr. Saunders of Grahamstown, given in the Municipal Congress this week, and the "Daily Dispatch" leader thereon, to say nothing of other public speakers and writers who figure frequently in newspapers. Secondly the negrophobists and repressionists too are by no means putting their candle underneath a bushel. They are becoming no less hardened in their venomous hate of the black man, as witnessed by their treatment of us in various spheres of life and in their writings, as for example in the Bloemfontein "Farmers' Weekly" and the "Homestead," where Native nurses and farm servants are vilified often in uncultured language.

Now what have we to say to all this? Are these two parties to remain our only advocates? No! I hope not. The time has come for us to work out our own salvation with our own instrumentality. To do so, we too must become more and more articulate, wisely articulate, specially in the press, and take all that is good in the white man's civilisation, eschewing the bad. The dangers that we should avoid are numerous, but I have selected a few and summed them under fourteen points, to follow the magic number of President Wilson, and shall now take them *seriatim*.

1. RELIGIOUS LAXITY.

1. The first one is Religious Laxity. By this I mean the growing slackness and deterioration in our hold on the religion bequeathed unto us by our parents and fore-fathers. From what we learn, the primitive Natives, though not religious in the modern sense of the word, were at least superstitious enough to have their moral life restrained by certain crude but nevertheless moral scruples. This was at any rate something of merit and credit to them, when one considers their little know-ledge of natural phenomena and the tendencies that made for moral depravity in those days. In the course of time Christianity was introduced and those of four generations ago received it truly and sincerely. The names of our earliest Native Missionaries still make us feel a glow of joy and pride in their excellent record of work in uplifting their people. Much work was done by their successors until missions are in many cases

so large now that most of our Missionaries—white and black—can find time to carry out only pastoral but no evangelising work. Considerable spiritual stagnation is apparent in the general church membership in municipal areas where the religion of many Natives consists only in church going and the observances of the outward form of Christianity, having no practical check to their moral actions. We are fast becoming Christians without religion! What a paradoxical position! Some plead that the whiteman too has no regard for his religion, for in Pretoria and elsewhere he goes in hundreds to the tennis courts, swimming baths, fishing and hunting expeditions on Sundays. But this is irrelevant, because two wrongs do not make a right. Let his white minister take care of the white man. We must not drift from the religion of our forbears for that is the cause of the prevalent dishonesty, untruthfulness and ruined characters among our people to-day. Therefore I say get back your religion from the Bible, not from the white man nor any other man; go back to the Church, back to God; or else there is the handwriting "Mene, Mene, Tekel, Upharsin," for we shall gain the world and lose our souls.

2. RACIALISM.

2. The second danger that I wish to deal with is that of racialism. By this I mean the feeling of hatred and contempt for other people for no other reason than that they belong to another tribe. Unfortunately we are being led in this despicable course by certain white men of standing in this land—doctors, clergymen and generals who are strong and influential racialists, so strong that they are contributing not a little to the general economic and political unsettlement of the Union. They have their prototypes amongst us

158

too, who are so strong in it that one would think they made a living out of it. So far as we are concerned racialism long ago was in certain senses a profitable thing, for our powerful chiefs used to favour men of their own clan at their courts, frequently presenting them with cattle and land in recognition for their obeisance (" ukubusa "). Conditions have changed since and racialism is now antiquated, mischievous and detrimental :—antiquated because our tribal communistic life is practically gone, having been supplanted by the magisterial system ; mischievous because it breeds jealousy and odium ; detrimental because it renders us mutually destructive in many a good thing we attempt. And this is just where the rise of evil lies in these celebrations ; these are liable to attach undue importance to harmless tribal differences in people of our stage of development. Therefore I exhort you to eliminate this motive of racial antipathy from your proceedings and let your whole attitude to people of other tribes and colours be one of generosity and love ; or else we shall be heading for certain disaster.

3. IGNORANCE.

3. I next take the danger of ignorance. You all know the saying that a little knowledge is a dangerous thing. Many of our people imagine that ignorance means only illiteracy and that once you have learnt to read and write you are no more ignorant but " educated." A greater mistake was never made. This is the very misconception that underlies most of the arguments used by some white people when they write to the press about Native servants, nurses and farm labour. The only ignorant Native with them is the one in the red blanket, otherwise they call educated any Native " in evidence on Sunday afternoons, when he swaggers up the street in his squeaky boots, jostling

passers-by, and carrying on a conversation with friends in broken English " (Loram). That is not education. You may remain densely ignorant even when you can read and pass some examinations. I am not going to speak about illiteracy for multitudes of you have passed beyond that stage. But we all need commonsense to enable us to create opportunities for ourselves. For example in one town I visited I met a black man who was a successful shoemaker. I asked him how he began life. He told me that at first he worked a long while for a European cobbler who paid him one pound a week, whereas when he counted up the shoes he actually repaired these were up to the value of four pounds and more. Disgusted with this state of things he left that shop, borrowed money from his uncle, opened his own business place, paid back the money within the very first week and was now earning five and six pounds a week for himself. This is the kind of knowledge you must develop: the knowledge of knowing what you can do with your strength and physical stamina with which the Creator has abundantly endowed the black people.

We must also resolve to be well-informed as to what is going on in this country and in the world. To remain in ignorance of the multifarious history-making events in the wide world and in this Union is to court disaster as well as to lose many blessings. As a proof of this let me say that the famous local Grey Hospital in which many of your lives have been saved, and which was bountifully granted to Native Africans by that memorable governor, Sir George Grey, was first cut in half for Europeans and a few weeks ago the Administrator decided to take it over in its entirety and convert it into a school for Europeans!!! Many of you do not know of this sinister dispossession adumbrated by our chief, Sir Frederic de Waal, at the instigation of your local authorities who often pride themselves on their sense of

160

justice towards their proteges, the Natives. Now as a result of your ignorance you have done nothing in the way of an organised protest. The Bechuana have a proverb that the child that does not cry dies on its mother's back. Why do you not cry out to your father the Government about this? Is it right? Is it British?

The papers also say that the Prime Minister is about to evolve local Advisory Councils for you or Bungas like that of the Transkei. Probably it will be a good thing. But how many of you know about it? What suggestion have you to make? Again the Administrator has foreshadowed a scheme of Free Education for us. Have you thanked him for it? Perhaps you do not know about that either. All these things fall upon you "like a bolt from a blue sky," and as a result of your ignorance you take no anticipative remedial measures. I recommend that you do less meat-eating in these celebrations and tackle these vital problems and thus save these people from impending ruin due to ignorance and lack of information.

My fourth point is the Petty Spirit or Narrowness. It is invariably associated with a smattering of education. It is sad to notice this spirit among our people in meetings connected with the church, or teachers, or location affairs. So-called leaders and many ministers are frequently to be found not taking the large and generous view of things to promote progress; but engaged in petty disputes with their sub-officers week after week, wasting valuable energy and eloquence in so doing. Hence schisms abound to-day in our churches, associations, political gatherings and in every sphere of life where black people are left to guide one another. Many spend much time in discussing and abusing the white man; in fact this has become the chief topic of our hot bloods around their firehearths of an evening.

Time is money, as the saying goes, and the day has come for us to use it more profitably than we have done heretofore, to do less negative criticism and more construction and to learn the white man's commercial methods that have given him his historical success. We should now look out for the good things of life and grasp them instead of inactively bemoaning our hapless lot in this land of our birth. Look at the celebrations in Grahamstown and the lofty educational aims and tangible objects aimed at by the descendants of those immigrants. In such celebrations as the Ntsikana and Abambo we should copy the deeds of those who are observing the Settlers' Centenary and emulate their practical objects. Watch the example of the Jews among us, how loyal they are to one another in everything they undertake. Learn from the achievements of the American Negroes whose labourers earn from fifteen to twenty shillings a day, for the same kind of unskilled work that you get two or three shillings a day for in this country. There is no difference between your physical strength and that of the Negroes, but they are organised while you are not, on account of your petty spirit. I pass on to the next point.

5. *The bad training of the young of our days.*—Most of us here were born in the hard old days when our parents strongly believed in the proverb "Spare the rod, spoil the child." Do you ever ask yourselves the pertinent questions: Why is it that there is so much insubordination and insolence in the young boys and girls of to-day as compared with our times? So much unreliability in the labour of our youth whether in town, in shops, in kitchens, in the farm, and in the training institutions? Can we entirely dispose of these questions in the easy way of blaming the white man?

Well, I put these questions straight to you because they were put to me last Christmas by white people of serious purpose, in round-table conferences in Johannesburg and East London and I had to explain it all on the spur of the moment.

It is agreed, wherever I ask the question, that the boys and girls of the present generation are far less amenable to discipline than those of ten years ago, and so on back to the date of our first contact with white men. Natives used to rely upon their tribal laws for maintaining discipline. The white man has compelled us to abandon our tribal system, and is now himself surprised at finding urban location boys, kitchen girls and farm labourers more difficult to manage. Unfortunately this is true for Native parents and Native employers too. Some parents have actually confessed to me that they are glad to get rid of their boys and despatch them to the training school or town as they are so unruly and such "hopeless cases" at home! These produce what is called the "spoilt Native" because they prove to be indolent and pig-headed in labour centres. One Native woman explained it by saying that the modern Native women greatly object to seeing their husbands whip the children ; and so they fly at their husband's throats whenever he attempts to castigate his boy for misconduct, the result of this parental wrangle producing in the boy contempt for elders, disrespect for authority and impudence towards employers. This question is a serious one for the whole of this country and such celebrations as these ought to ponder over these difficulties, using as a basis of discussion a book like "Umzi Ontsundu" (the Native People) by Brownlee Ross, who lucidly examines the effects of the process of Native detribalisation.

6. *Educational Needs.*—As the report of the Native Education Commission is not yet published one cannot tell how far our needs have been met, nevertheless, I wish to draw your attention to the fact that our present

163

educational system has the effect of giving us stones instead of bread. For example it leaves out Hygiene, Cookery and Agriculture.

When I visited the Negro schools in America in 1913, I found that lessons on hygiene were given to children from the lowest classes to the highest. In this land hundreds leave school every year without having had a single lesson on the elementary facts of health, healthy habits or therapeutics. This could be done very easily because the Lovedale "Health Society" under Dr. Macvicar, has numerous publications on the subject in Xosa, Suto, Chwana and Zulu which could be supplied to all our elementary and training institutions at very small cost. It is up to you to move in these matters and get the school managers to do these things for you.

Take Cookery, a thing which ought to be known by all our girls without exception. I frequently receive letters from anxious parents who wish for advice as to schools where their girls could be trained in Cookery and Domestic Science. Knowing of no such school in the Cape Province I usually refer them to Indaleni, Natal, where it is said this is done. It is this defective training for the necessities of life that renders thousands of our Native female teachers so woefully ignorant of the simplest elements of house-keeping. Our schools should undertake this, but it is for you to tell the Education Department about it in no uncertain language and to worry them until they do it.

What could be more profitable for our boys, for ourselves and for the country than the training of our boys in Agriculture? In Tuskegee Institute, Alabama, U.S.A., I found that although there were forty vocational industries taught, including the Science of Agriculture, yet every boy was compelled to take the elementary course in agriculture (just as every girl had to take the Domestic Course) irrespective of the trade they were learning. I must at this point confess that although I was trained in the British Empire, and in a University inferior to none on earth, yet in the elementary vocational education I discovered that Booker Washington, the American Negro, had far more commonsense than all the English tradition-ridden educationists that I know of. The practical influence of his education system in Alabama and throughout the United States in wonderful. It is for us then to give our Government no rest until they provide us too with agricultural training. Personally I would prefer to see American Negro agricultural experts, or failing these, Natives of this land, taught American agriculture, dotted all over this country in our Native Training Schools, teaching agriculture to our boys. A sympathetic and well-educated black man can do a great deal to inspire our people to great things in the line of agriculture. Let us therefore ask the Government for these things. Ask and it shall be given unto you. Our great sin is that of *not* asking. These three subjects would be far more useful to us than the present Sewing, Drawing and Woodwork classes that prove utterly useless to our boys and girls in after school life.

You should commemorate your celebrations also by granting scholarships to promising pupils; and I may inform you that there are four students at our College enjoying £10 scholarships tenable for four years in consequence of representations I made to some kind and Christian people in England. You should do the same for your race. You should have a fund to help and encourage writers like Mqayi, Sigila, Pelem, Bokwe, J. S. Mazwi and many others who hold manuscripts of books on Native matters awaiting printing, books which will do much for our education and edification. These tasks are heavy for one man, but light if undertaken by many.

7. DISEASE.

My seventh subject is the alarming spread of diseases, dangerous and infectious diseases, among Native people. These are many : but the most conspicuous perhaps are 1. Tuberculosis or Consumption, 2. Infantile Mortality, 3. Venereal diseases, 4. Enteric fever, 5. Influenza and Pneumonia, 6. Typhus, and 7. Small-pox.

As I am not a medical man I do not propose to expatiate on these diseases but only to draw your attention (a) to the huge numbers of people these claim in all our Native districts, (b) to the frightful figures of the death rate of children to be seen in statistics thereanent, (c) to general comments made by doctors, (d) to literature which we should all read carefully, and (e) to practical steps that we should undertake to counteract the ravages of these diseases and thereby to save our Native race from what may palpably be regarded as threatening us with ultimate extermination.

Census figures tell us a good deal of the rapid increase of the Bantu population but little of the dread diseases that are killing it off. Enlightened Natives should study these figures carefully and they will be horrified at the facts.

Our death rate is about double that of Europeans, and the story told by Dr. Macvicar of Lovedale, in his thesis on "Tuberculosis" (price 1/-) is painful reading, because hundreds of our people die each year mainly from their ignorance of the methods of fighting the "white man's scourge." See also the remarks made by Dr. Saunders of Grahamstown, at the Municipal Congress. Consult also the Union Year Book (3/-) and the Report of the Housing Commission where we are told

that while on the average about 70 to 90 European
infants die in a thousand, the rate for Natives ranges
between 240 in the King Williamstown district to 543
in Pretoria! Think what that means. It means that
Native babies die so heavily in some places that only
one in two, or less, stands the chance to survive. Do
these figures not make you shudder? Can we not do
something to help our benighted people? Must we
wait until eternity for the white man's generosity and
not save ourselves?

White people have organised into societies for the
protection of Child Life and they have clever lecturers
like Dr. Elsie Chubb to go round teaching white mothers
the science of child rearing while we, with an infant
death-roll five times as heavy, are unorganised and are
left to ourselves.

Again venereal diseases like syphilis are so common
that a white lady speaker in Johannesburg recently
made the grave statement that Native nurse-maids
should not be trusted with white children as they are
mostly rotten and reeking with this contagion and that
among Natives there is no morality, as Europeans understand the word. Are these things true?

What have you to say in defence? Watch also the
other infectious diseases like typhoid, influenza, typhus,
small-pox and many more which are carrying off
hundreds of the Bantu people of South Africa. It is
time people in general were warned against these
diseases and taught how to avoid them and how to treat
them when striken with them. I would strongly recommend all of you at this celebration to make a beginning
by writing to the Secretary of the "Health" newspaper
at Lovedale, and send three pennies for any of the
following pamphlets which may be had in the vernacular languages—singly or all in one book costing
7d. post free, thus 1. Umtshetsha Pantsi (The Prevention

167

of Scurvy), 2. The Prevention of Consumption, 3. Inya-
niso nge Alcohol, 6. How Consumption spreads in
Families, 7. Tuberculosis Catechism, 8. Public Health,
9. Communicable Diseases, 11. Houses and Health,
12. Malarial Fever, 13. Syphilis, 14. Enteric Fever,
15. Advertised Medicines, 16. Feeding of Babies, 17.
Anti-Consumption Cartoon in English, Xosa, Zulu,
Sesuto.

Lastly, what steps should we take to have more native
medical practitioners amongst us? The need for native
properly trained doctors is very great now for there are
thousands of Natives who live beyond the reach of
white doctors in our country villages. For instance
between Alice and King Williamstown (46 miles by
rail) five doctors are needed but there is not one available. At present I know of only four native doctors
trained in Scotland, namely, Dr. Mahlangeni in the
Transkei, Dr. Sebeta in Basutoland, Dr. Moroka in
Thaba Nchu and Dr. Molema in Mafeking. We need
hundreds for many of the white ones no longer care to
deal with natives, some will not do it at all, others
examine natives in stables !

The case for the need of Native doctors has been
eloquently put by Dr. J. B. McCord and Dr. C. T. Loram
in the African Journal of Science, January, 1919. In
pursuance of this object there is a movement on foot
in the King Williamstown district to raise money to
educate a native through Edinburgh University on the
two conditions that he, when qualified, return to practise in the district that sent him, and to charge reasonable fees. This is the kind of thing your celebration
should fittingly undertake and by which you could
benefit not only yourselves but the whole black race.

8. ALCOHOLISM.

My next point is the curse of alcoholism which is
probably the most destructive engine that European

civilisation has inflicted us with. It requires a number of lectures by itself, though I have made some remarks on it in my address to Native teachers in Natal. Think of how it has undermined some of the best brains among our leading Natives and rendered them incapable of discharging the momentous responsibilities that their ability, influence and education had led all of us to anticipate from them. Remember the words of King Khama of Bechuanaland, who when opposing strong drink in his land twenty-five years ago said, "I fear Lobengula less than I fear the white man's drink. To fight against drink is to fight against demons, not against men. The assegais of the Matabele kill men's bodies, and it is quickly over; but drink puts devils into men and destroys both their souls and their bodies for ever."

Our great difficulty is that multitudes of our people copy the bad example of our leading men who drink. I know of many Native chiefs, teachers, ministers of the the gospel, and men who have the School Higher and Matriculation certificates who, by succumbing to this evil are responsible for leading astray thousands of innocent young lives, some of whom I have seen intoxicated in the railway trains as they travel to and from training institutions. The dangers of alcohol even in its mildest doses should be taught to children from the very lowest classes to the highest that we have. The Temperance leagues need to make more of the physiological than the moral harm of alcohol. A system of public lectures with illustrated lantern slides upon the effects of alcohol on the human body would go a long way to counter-act mischievous fallacies on alcohol spread by those interested in the trade and readily believed by our gullible and untutored people.

9. IMPROVIDENCE.

In the days of our forefathers it was the ambition of every man to own cattle and to have ploughing land.

To-day this is impossible for manifold reasons: stock is dying through new diseases and lack of pasturage; we work for wages and salaries, whilst many of us are born and bred in urban locations where stock ownership is impracticable. We have to learn the European ways of saving. Opportunities abound but it is remarkable how hundreds of Natives die every year leaving only debts for their widows and little children, there being no money even to pay for their coffins and burial, and this after having worked in town for ten or twenty years. You should all study the various ways of saving money; study the Banks and the Post Office Saving Bank, Building Societies, Life Insurances, Union Loan Certificates, Property Insurance, Fire Insurances, etc., and invest part of your wages in them. For instance you can out of your wages of 15/- a week put 6d. into an Industrial Life Assurance Society, which will at your death give your widow £50 cash down; a 1/- a week gives £100 and so on. It is very easily done. You may join a Property Insurance too which in six years' time buys you a house or a farm of your own, and instead of paying rent to a landlord or interest to a bondholder for thirty years for property that will never be yours, pay interest to your society which will gradually diminish your capital until in thirty years' time the house or farm becomes yours outright. I once persuaded a servant of mine to bank part of his monthly wages of a sovereign in the Post Office Bank. Some months he put in very little but nevertheless something, and at the end of twelve months when he left me he drew £4 in red gold and bought a heifer which has since multiplied for him into three cattle! Now I know for certain that many of you looking at me right now have not a penny in your name in any bank although you get between 15s. and 25s. a week. This is a crying shame. Make up your minds from now not to allow a single week or month to pass without

170

saving something. I know of one man in East London who put in 2s. 6d. a week in his bank and even borrowed it of others when he was penniless and in a short time he had pounds and pounds to his credit. To allow a month or a year to pass by without its showing something saved or some insurance investment maintained is in my view a positive sin!

(It may here be mentioned that on the morning following the delivery of this address several young men who had listened to it actually opened up new bank accounts and proudly came to report that to the lecturer).

10. INDEBTEDNESS.

Have you ever devoted a thought to the great depths into which our poople are sinking through debt? If I could spend half an hour telling you the result of my observations on this within a fifty mile radius—you would not believe. You would say that it is merely the romance of an imaginative mind. Anyhow I shall not give you concrete illustrations as these may be seized by malicious creatures and used or abused for their own ends. Suffice it to say the owing of debts to traders and lawyers by our people has grown so common that it is reckoned fashionable, and people talk quite boldly and brazenly about their debts to other people. They think it no shame. This evil has been brought about by successive years of drought together with high prices following the World War. We must all put our shoulder to the wheel and fight the evil if we mean to liberate our countrymen from the grinding pincers of the prevailing economic distress. Our people must be taught that it is wrong and shameful to go into or remain in debt when they have the opportunity to keep out of it. No native enslaved by debt can hope to rise to independence of thought and morality.

171

11. LOW WAGES.

Our indebtedness is largely explained by the smallness of our wages. The money we are paid does not cover the cost of our barest necessities. At East London a Native labourer has to pay about 30s. a week for such strict necessaries of life as food, rent, paraffin, wood, etc., while the average pay is 22s.; and this leaves no margin for the purchase of boots, hats, shirts, clothes, nor savings and many other items indispensable to a town man. And yet the commercial men express surprise at the fact that the municipal native is growing dishonest and thievish. Stealing is the wrong way of solving this problem. The right way, the white man's way, is organisation. You should learn to form trades unions of your own, led by intelligent people, and to act as one man when asking for an increase in wages. Your employers at present laugh at you because they know that they hold the whip over you. If you leave them there are hundreds of others as good as yourselves ready to jump into your places just because you are not organised. In my opinion organisation, intelligent organisation, is your only hope to receive wages commensurate with the present advanced cost of living.

12. WRONG FOODS.

The introduction of European foods has led many of our people to drop the bone and catch at the shadow. They seek after coffee, tea, rice, sugar, while utterly despising porridge, curdled milk (amasi) and (umvubo), the medley of ground mealie bread with curdled milk. They do not like green vegetables which are to be found in great variety in the fields, fourteen species at least being found in my district. The consequences are that the race is deteriorating, scurvy is on the increase, and teeth are bad. Experts tell us that the purpose of food is to form

172

flesh, impart heat, create strength, enrich blood and form bone; we need in our diet to have starch, fats, vegetables and amasi. Our people need to be taught these things, to be taught that tea and coffee are *not* foods but only beverages stimulating the nervous system, increasing perspiration and the action of the heart, and producing insomnia or sleeplessness.

Specially that tea-leaves if allowed to remain in the teapot for over three minutes give out tannin poison that produces indigestion, constipation, nervousness and sleeplessness. Rice has no nourishing value, instead of it we should eat maize and kafircorn. The food question needs our careful study.

13. BAD FARMING.

On this I would prefer to give a separate lecture. Enough here for me to say that our first task is to convince our people that they stand in need of learning new facts about the science of agriculture. Next, to teach the methods of Dry Farming so that people shall cease to excuse their failure in agriculture by enumerating excuses like the lack of rain, the scorching sun and poor condition of cattle. They must be taught the "gelesha" system of the preparation of the soil, to educate their sons at the Tsolo Agricultural School or at Mariannhill, Natal, or at the S. A. Native Collge, Fort Hare, and lastly, to organise associations purely for agriculturists where they should discuss their problems and ask government for demonstrators.

14. POVERTY.

My 14th and last point is *Poverty*. It is about time that we combined our forces to fight and drive away this wolf from our doors. Poverty is responsible for many enormities among us. It has made many of our people

173

thieves and wicked men, has made them leave the salubrious countryside for the towns where they are ill housed; it has brought the contempt of Europeans upon our social life, making everything that belongs to a black man an object of amusement (e.g. our ragged and tattered garments, our dilapidated dwelling houses, furniture, church buildings and even hymn books). It has made it impossible for us to attain stability in business, churches, politics, congresses, education and organisation.

Picture to your minds what we could be if we had more of this world's goods: how we could educate our sons and daughters to the utmost of their intellectual capacity, how we could enlarge and improve our schools, multiply high schools in every province and develop the Native College to its true ideal of the Mecca of Native Education, how by bettering ourselves economically we could compel the admiration and respect of all other races and gain our true political status in the government of this land. All these privileges belong to us but are denied us just because of our impotent ignorance and poverty, and we shall continue to be the bottom dog until we make a serious effort to overtake our white neighbours who owe their omnipotence to their education and wealth.

Ladies and gentlemen, I am not being carried away by flights of imagination and fantasy when I say that in my mind I can picture a time coming within a few ages from now when a great change will come over the Bantu races, when our posterity shall reach yet undreamt-of heights in the arts of civilisation, if we but conscientiously discharge the duties that belong to our present epoch, if we bequeath unto them sure foundations whereon to build their educational, religious, moral and political structure. When I was in America I was privileged to behold as if in a dream, the achievements of the Negroes in culture—to enjoy life in their palatial Negro hotels in Montgomery, their capacious four-storeyed edifices in Birmingham (Alabama) used by negro doctors, lawyers and insurance companies, the beautiful Negro theatres and Y.M.C.A. quarters in Washington and New York, their picturesque colleges at Tuskegee and Howard staffed and governed by Negroes only, wealthy Negro merchants in their automobiles, their stupendous church organisations in Georgia—all this fired my soul to believe that there were no altitudes in civilisation outside the compass of a black-skinned man if he only have the inspiration and determination to attain thereunto. Let us therefore strive to accomplish what is expected of this generation, so that in that beautiful future when the Bantu race is weighed in the balances it shall, thanks to our efforts, not be found wanting.